# Poetry
# New Zealand
# Yearbook

**2020**

# Poetry
# New Zealand
## Yearbook
### 2020

Edited by Johanna Emeney

MASSEY UNIVERSITY PRESS

# Contents

# Editorial

# How the poems choose you

It is wonderful to be chosen by poems, and the very opposite of trying to choose poems. Choosing poems is hard work — it feels like rifling through perfectly serviceable clothes from a stockier, taller cousin. Being chosen by poems, however, is like winning a voucher from your favourite shop and being dressed by one of its very genial and talented personal assistants. The poems that choose you are must-have items.

Poems choose you when they howl without any sort of dissembling — and yet a howl is not necessary. Pain is not even a prerequisite. However, sincerity is integral to a poem's ability to single you out as its guardian. Any sign of fraudulence, and it's all off. When a poem says 'but motherfucker' to you in entreaty or complaint, it better not be playing around — see essa may ranapiri's 'my dream of a nonbinary prison' for an example.

A poem chooses you the moment it takes you by surprise. To be clear, this cannot be any old surprise. It must have the qualities of what President Oprah Winfrey calls the 'A-ha moment' — a sudden insight which causes the pulse to quicken and galvanic skin temperature to rise. A poem like this is no riddle; it is a messenger imparting a truth about what it is to be human in the world. In fact, it probably touches on something you have already felt or secretly known, but never quite been able to admit.

Some poems don't need electrodes to test your bodily response. Paula Harris's poem brought me to tears on first reading. And second. Interestingly, it has some very humorous lines as well as some that agitate the lacrimal glands, and I am always in awe of poets who can produce this sort of work — poetry that blends fresh, funny lines with lines that expose the abject difficulty of being alive. It's the sort comedy–pathos amalgam that Jimmy Perry and David Croft achieved in *Dad's Army*, Larry Gelbart achieved in *M\*A\*S\*H*, and Ricky Gervais and Stephen Merchant achieved in *The Office*. Although they were working with made-up characters, and surely, by now, everybody knows that the poet *is* the 'I' of the poem. Wink emoji.

Because I am editing, and not writing, the poetry in this journal, I feel free to say: 'Poems that choose you are like *mille-feuilles* — thoughtfully assembled and subtly layered', which is a simply dreadful simile, but very true in terms of the type of poems I am describing. Whether those layers come by way of diction, imagery, mood or nuance, it doesn't matter, but if you can't get a few readings out of a poem because it's a one-trick cupcake, then you're wasting your time. Michael Hall's 'Fencing' is a superb example of a compact poem with deftly constructed layers. It is a poem that will reward you with new insights every time you read it. The last stanza is fabulously dense, with its metaphor of the father and son tacking down the backdrop to a day:

> Some days he tightened
> The horizon
> And started hammering
> As I held the staple in place

*Why does the son only appear in this last stanza? The son seems so small here in relation to his father! But, wait, he is steadying the staple — the thing that holds the horizon tightly in place once his father has hammered it in . . . so he is key to this whole enterprise. The son may be just the staple-holder, but he is his father's right-hand-man here, helping him to hold the whole world in place (as fathers do, for a time).* So many thoughts triggered by four lines, and we have not even addressed the sounds of the lines as Hall works them like fencing wire, lengthening, tightening and tacking.

It has been a privilege, this year, to be chosen by so many moving, well-crafted poems written by people I know well and people I have never met. What a pleasure to be introduced to so many talented poets this way. I am grateful to Jack Ross and the team at Massey University Press for the opportunity, and for their guidance and trust.

# Featured Poet

## essa may ranapiri

# HAUNT | HUNT

## poetry under capitalism

i'm hitting wooden blocks together
and finding shapes to fit the holes of everyone's mouths
and everyone's hopes of usefulness
in a perfect sheer drop
corpses rubbing cobwebs together

# my dream of a nonbinary prison

as of this moment Aotearoa has no nonbinary prisons
no unisex facilities for people like me          I can almost
taste the toilet soap          and hear the fragrant stream
of water slapping the steel          wall of the urinal
if not for the symbols          on the door

my tūpuna would be so proud          of how many
have made it          to these fine estates
living on the land          in the only way we know how
weaving makeshift harakeke from          matted paper rolls
we dried with     tooth paste          and snot
carving intricate geometry          into the metal bars

I have no place          in the entire nation state
where I can be clothed and fed          for the simple price
of my freedom          and my dignity
if I push my phone          far enough up my
arsehole you'll never          be able to touch it
and I'll never have to          call my family again

these closed spaces          would bring me to

P                                        R     n          g
     a                                        a               i
               p                    n
                    a     &              u
          t                              i
     ū     ā     n
          u
               k     u
churned up inside          a gigantic mixer
returned to each other          their love cemented at last
                                        in the walls

then washed over:

                              brick painted white
                        wallpaper painted white
                           a face painted white
                       knuckles painted white
                                painted white
                                panting white
                               witness white
                   judge jury executive white

        but motherfucker

there is no place where I can be forced into a single cell
for the benefit of my mental health
be taught my own tikanga free of charge where I can run
bitten fingernails over the hem of the plastic mat

there is no safe

                                        place for me

        to die as a criminal

## that flaming brand

the light was only ever a sword
was only ever a fire to take my skin
from me

the car wrapped around a pole at the
centre of the milky way

## the world is in death swings

insistence gutted on silly putty
pledge add me to buzz saw sounds
and breach the stable
the stallions and mares and geldings
are whinnying in the dusk
scared of a red coat attack
it's a spread-their-troops-thin kind of summer

the hazel Hephaestus slumbers in the hottest of pits
hiding hammers inside his chest
limping through Vesuvius soil
press cold hands to the environmental statues
mountains bowed to human shapes

the reaching out
that speaking out
and visibility
are more net tangled
in a biohazard
suit
and the poisonous weeds
and the lasting train wreck

the tracks make a gentle shadow
on the fence

## a cold sting

you tried to find
a jar filled with
frozen bees
each one dead
so i could write a poem about it
but upon opening
the freezer
there was only a box
with your supervisor's name
on it
and none of her bees
inside

## by the grace of god

Was the page plucked from Providence? All up out from Providence? A flesh dream with an ill look, with people's hands on so many swords, a mouth, a gaze, a dry cut the smallest of holes in the newspaper from where the printing press stabbed it. Are these what we call standards?

Can my matter be not natural can my matter skin happiness alive?

I am free of fire. From blood the Article. Eden waiting. Forced to leave but stays. Money and mouth touch the table, leave it for bigger hands: collect a whole load and shiver from the weight.

## swimming

I am stuck
in a cavern made of cotton
check-marked
everything I wanted to see in
the basin of who I am
oh
it glistens all over in the slit
for light

worms swimming in
globes that cling to
greys smather over blacks
swaddle me
in shiver
swaddle me in suffer
swaddle
me in sibilance

I can smell it take up space
and continue to take up space
like a dreadball weight wrapped in
cellophane

## intimacy

in the retail of my spine
this form of lip and bristle and grit
assembles an army of cells
each amoeba scuttles across the ocean floor
and clambers through the froth of broken water
to reach the apex
bucktooth
quartz
of your laughter

**it is what these words tell me daily**
**it is what they need from me that hurts the most**

imagine the abattoir
gunmetal blood-shiny
imagine the brain
a soft muscle
loose-thread patch balled
not good with pressure

we have a new non-stick pan
so the cooking is easier
but it doesn't go down easier

### *you tried to kill yourself*

through two locked doors
sliding apart before a card and a carer leading us
an exception in visiting times
there you are after three hours of bullshit
the wait the drive the wait

my father:

greying curls

speckled stubble

face gone gaunt

whatever fat melted off

and eyes that open only so much

a V stitched into the neck

corded lines straight down

track pants

polyester

split down the side

left side

feet bare

just sitting there just sitting there just sitting there

pallid with a yellow tinge
there is a black spot above your left eye
folding up against your brows

right arm in a cast

what a commitment
it fills the air like a rock

I shake my head
up and down and wait with nothing to say
as you pour out

start to move the chairs around the room
why are there so many seats under a white light
push them to the edge to hug the wall

all movement is unnatural here
I see the wireframe stretched through you
to hold you back

while you tell me from your position of never being there

that

*Love is such a vague word*

## my tupuna / jesus of nazareth

they carried eyes for me before my birth that swivelled
and pointed north                                  in the dark
you                                couldn't see that scorcher
couldn't have known what it brought to the people
to the real people of the dark places                te pō
bring the manna into the basement of my body        from
te kore                        they wrote my gender all wrong
a *he* inside the blue-balled g-d                they made it
to the temple and soaked their fat in the fabric of the city
you must be making rules to make money                follow
that herder into the gap made by the quaking earth
people turning out confused by the presence of other
people with no job to do                they fucked as they
always did elizabeth and john inside the face of g-d
so infinitely sombre in their touching like a cut and dash
like a fade to black no cumshot in the presence of my
dad or mum or both let's right us a            genderqueer g-d
they ride bodies in seclusion and teach each other how to
tie all kinds of laces here and there in the citadel —
glorified spit or a mummified spirit merely made for
grasping at the higher grapes merely made for squashing
the fallen gape the sun came out of her womb i saw it
and it looked like an older version of me — there is a
mercy in our ancestors that just has no currency here —
augustus called out for every person to be marked down

but how many was i? an echo of            he he he he
cackle false gender            trying to put on me i came
out in the town of david my fragile ancestor my futile
connection            i whakapapa to a nuclear meltdown
i whakapapa to an expanse of empty and an expanse of
dark            the pinpoint they cut the skin from
i got straw in my hair i swam the exegesis became a
mottled lisp brooms scraping my dark skin my rich
scales — she mops the floor in a hot flush i can feel the
fire in the cleaning supplies — it don't do much to the
overall atmosphere of the place i should think            my
nature missing link      medea crawling the earth for her
babies stenched flush            level of drench my
sight is sludgy as my soul connects back to the harness as
its demons play poker in the steam of my underbelly
oh my wairua my holy ghost creeping back to the tip of
the tail            titans fighting the mincemeat of the
clouds the rich scented disaster of ambrosia a greek
drama    disappearing    in    the    lack    of    copyright
my            body            receding            into
the      peaceful      depths      of      mistranslation

## Boulder/Meteor

please don't say it's got anything to do with
mobiles clinking in the wind        breeze will
scatter sound i swear it will      make a promise
let the bug down from the tree      how did
it get so high      made a milkbud cave
made a crumb into a kingdom with just one
mouth      i stare at the austerity what a policy to
give us wings to fall from      what mud slick
dinosaur prays for metcors every night      the
stars could be so much bigger i know      i really
do    please    don't    stay    you    won't
like what you see      two magnets pressed
together on the wrong sides everything of great
size started out smaller than the human eye could
recognize      if i glue these two pebbles
together and add dirt everyday for a thousand
years would i have the boulder needed to crush
everything we've done wrong      would i be
adding to it      megalomania is only mania if
you're wrong      and i promise please leave
the element going with the pot empty of water to
run to hot hot      please please leave

## the carpenter

myrmidon with thorax rub and skitter of segmented legs
with mandibles made of . . .

they cannot eat the wood or any solid form of plant
matter but chew through the walls of your house to make
a home a thin tunnel of paper writing a new form of
scripture that is milked from aphids and pushed into the
child's mouth
such a small failing sweet as holy shit
                              for the brain to jungle
and make food with the liquids as an ink drip

## in the shade

You didn't like the way I looked at Your apples
so I found a good place in the shade
away from Your throne

everything You throw — into the Garden
tastes the same; a porridge of salt and gristle
the complexity sterilized on a canvas sheet
it slops through in molten heaps
feed into trough to separate from the shine

You keep the rest for Your estate
brittle material to build a mansion
that punctures the night
not darker than the lightbulb filament
of a giant's eye straining

when You couldn't find me
You began to pin animals to the Earth
where I watched through a telescope
a constellation of rusted tacks in meat
globes of red budding from every entry wound

away from the violence
waiting in the gorse
for rose petals to rain down
onto the lens
I watch the whole thing play out like
looking is some substitute for a full stomach.

## took their solitary way

I find Her lying in the water
with the wairua of my tupuna
She is braiding their hair and brushing pīwakawaka
feathers over their eyes. She looks at me and draws my
nose to Hers. I cough, and it echoes in the cave
of my chest. There doesn't seem to be any
break between motions. She pushes a hand through my
rib cage bone recognizing bone moving apart
to the red meat of my heart. Makes art of its pump
with obsidian finger-nails. Cardiac massage to keep me.
My body finally a house I can recognize and love!
Her hand is callouses to close me up. Wishing to
be as hard as Her. But I melt like marshmallow on the
stick or glad-wrap in the oven. Never as useful as I
would like but
    so so warm.

## Modern-day Poi

we scrunched old newspapers
and squeezed them into plastic-bag
parachutes
(New World still clear
on the cut up squares) worked them
until balled-up
tied off at the end with wool (black
and red strands braided together) i would
always have trouble with the knot required
to hold it all, strips of obituary
and letter to the editor
trailing through the gaps i had carelessly
left breathing
i remember the feeling as they swung from
my hands in ever increasing rotations
until the speed blurs the fragile
structure to ruins
a piece of paper thrown across the room

## General Electric as an All-Powerful Immortal Being

125 years old     counting
up & up     with no care for
the ages     it has taken     bodies
it puts inside its own body     that
can only know     expansion
tumorous bulges     in the living room
in the kitchen     fingers scattering through
cereal boxes     to rest legs in the tarmac

you husk you homunculus you storm of flesh
   you're kicking out     moving from
Connecticut     to Boston
am I happy for you     to hold
so many people inside your belly
to give them a purpose     to take part
in the economy
the car gets scratched on the way
to work wear     battle scars
in the paint

oh great and power     full god
of aviation, obsolescence, energy connections,
stethoscopes, halogen lights, oil and gas,
deity of the growl of trains, life sciences,
benzodiazepines,
sweat on the brow, carpal tunnel, ptsd
and capital;

bone soup reduced and
frozen in an ice cube tray
take your stock push it into a ravine
does your

reach
know
no
bounds

you built the reactors        can you remember doing
that
building them cheap        a smaller design to create
fireworks
you thought they would be so pretty when the wave hit
pulling cities back out to float in the sea

and you were right of course      make everything
to break
because it's only natural for things to die     early
there is a wire twisted in a way so that as it shakes
the rest of its circuits to dust    you can spend as much
or as little as you want the exchange of goods and
services for cash
is another type of speech
when your mouth moves like the ding of cash registers
you tongue the golden arches of fast food
lolling to a stop as spit slides down the graphs
your recessive trait
is to bring everything with you
when you die next time will the state insert a nasogastric
tube

                    and pump you full
with those *words*     sweet greens to nurse you back to
health
endlessly
or will you
have the guts to collapse under your weight

## the end of Hawaiki

did they find oil there
the big blustery Americans
with their drones
and their hard-won red
necks
folding in
to look at the dirt underneath
the nails as something to wash
down the drain

the whales are bigger here than anywhere else
one man said to the other
before cutting
them open for their fat
we can power a whole state with this
shit
keep the cars running for another year

the traffic piling up on highways made of smoke

## our future is cancelled

*being trans-feminine under male gaze*

cords of muscle
draped in the codes of a million hungry men
*not at all hungry*
for the prickle when the paper will do.

a bucket of milk for the twisted ankle
what kind of vessel
for the twisted side
and that lump of coal

you call the heart
when you don't want to give in

*being earth under blaze*

the lungs deforested have
crisp shade of laughter
trapped in the arch of the throat
a beaver dam

business to harbour
docked in the tradition of sinking ships
*i wouldn't do it otherwise.*

running out of luck

the old arm is crunched against the side
couldn't get a grip on

that terrible
prize
it just keeps slipping

a painted plastic duck
marked and scribbled out

drivers flocking
oil in the mouth
gargled it sticks like a problem but it's not a
problem
it's how it goes
that waiting around second
(could use the image of a clock here)
but i don't

*being nothing more than the last syllable before the full stop*

O the swirl of the solar system
it is a plummet

# Headline

what could possibly fix what is happening — Israel Establishes Apartheid Regime — Texas Senate Passes Controversial Bathroom Bill SB6 — EU workplace headscarf ban legalized — Family remember 5-year-old killed in South LA hit-run — Trump puts brakes on vehicle emission targets — I have a huge commitment to staying in the world — Woman, 19, killed by train while trying to launch a modelling career — if you truly love — US to get $77b defence boost — Economy comes off the boil — Algae turns beaches neon blue — me then you would stay here with your feet planted in the soil of this fucked up earth — Hand cramp led to worker's death — Two suicide bombers have killed at least 39 people in the Syrian capital, Damascus. — Vet survives bite by deadly snake — until it sinks into the heat-death we all want — Mila, former NZ circus elephant who made headlines for killing her handler, has died in US — Austria avalanche kills three — Assange decision delayed — 114 new planets discovered — and none of them is going to save us

## borrowed blue pale dead

I can feel the arguments in their throats
like lost sparrows barrowing up, my birds
are spitting, a feathered façade, a paddling
pool for dislocated pumps. A whole crowd.
I am fingering the valves and trying to tighten
the passages with my flesh. Currency loaded into
the punchline of your headline. Badump badump bad
like how a candle flame flickers. Skin is like a kind of
string to pluck — remove the outer layer like music. Fold
them into flowers — a petal to consume — hold down
right next to your tonsils. Optical illusion as metaphor
and hyperreality as code to live by as coda. A creature-
fear blowing at the back of your neck. The necks of trees
exposing rings to the stars. Silent voice box inside the
stumps — sprouting sounds. Trash compactor. Metal
din. There are no things that can hurt you outside.
Outside of these walls the body of the world is
undergoing post-mortem. A dead rock with projections
of respiration. Stab teeth into a microphone and
feedback ourselves. The crowd is silent except for a
creaking in the throats like old rigging hitting the side of
a flagship. Pretending it's floating is the same as *it is
floating* right? The eye sound in die and lie is the same.

## out/ or not out

no i
i think so
just this
how could you use this

it was the right decision

decision cocooned
i see now

losing me

something important
something that catches the light
in such a way you can still see through it

i love you

something that bursts from a pip somewhere

i mean it

## Restless Land (after Dinah Moengarangi Rawiri's 'The Resting Islands')

Pale seas we lived long enough
to gaze upon   all birdsong dimmed
a muffling down to tortured throat noise
traffic jam grimaces     the roads are narrowed
by populace     everything fanged everything
insidiously noted-down everything flattened beneath
slates of pink-grey kauri
still sticky blood-sore     they put down the
seed     hungry and hungry and hungry for
the land to crawl back into the ocean where
it belongs to pale minds painted over
and full of fear
they know what they are
ferret and stoat in their soul
stomach full of feathers.

## loveletterunderdarkness

I

it's late & ur crying at the end of things or just because
something ends: a song; a poem; a year; idling vehicles
chipping paint on crosses. nightlight with bulb dangling
like a life that has been too kind, u put it all in greyscale
to save printing money. the last line clean red slit across
(where the base of the jaw meets the neck proper) u r sorry
for being so far away (nt sry). how can u tell which note
to end on, not a real question, the joints get brittle the
healthy launch of air from knuckle from joint in pinky,
u don't think there is anywhere to hide. the metaphors
for death come easy, just finding another word for fun
is so difficult (slots into funeral like a lego piece!) o what
do u hear in between the gap after the song has finished
and the next, not a real question, there is nothing

## II

i think about pinching your hips, a quiet prod. nails
making pink sickles, communist propaganda in the white
lightning of ur stretch-marks. how fast is growing up too
fast, not a real question, i think uve got the drill by now.
'none of us are free till all of us are free,' — i am only
here because someone else loves me enough. this is more
than just some thing or anything. u fall asleep dreaming
of trains; i have a dream where two toddlers all gums and
snot, are fighting over the tattered remains of a black
balloon; my uncle, fibreglass dust brushing his collar, is
trying in vain to get my name right; i want everyone in
the room to die with me. not real but it begs the
question, do i grow in my sleep or just shrink

III

would i follow u where-ever u go, not a real question but
it is a real question someone like me could hold in their
gut. could i rule one-thousand estates from across the
seas. no i must just be a figment of someone's
imagination. lie down on unmade bed, duvet scattered,
mattress spotty with blood, dried months ago, to smell ur
biome lingered. how long is a song if u have nothing to
measure it with, rhetorical, how long is any of this going
to last, two bodies (if we're keeping score) floating in and
out of the event horizon. nothing and then something
and then

## An interview with essa may ranapiri

essa may ranapiri (Ngāti Raukawa) began writing poetry when they were 14, penning lyrics that they didn't know were poetry for a guitar that they claim still to be learning. Despite that rather equivocal start, they graduated from the International Institute of Modern Letters' MA programme in 2017 and published *ransack*, their first poetry collection, with Victoria University Press in July 2019.

Now 26, essa is anything but equivocal. They have an unshakeable quality of knowing who they are and where they stand, which is very comforting to witness. It is something like confidence, but more hard-won. It is something that comes across in essa's poems, even when they express absolute despair. Perhaps the only way to describe it is self-certainty.

I saw essa read at the Wellington Writers Festival in 2018. I had gone with my friend Ros Ali to watch Sophie van Waardenberg, one of our Young Writers Programme alumnae, perform as part of the Flock of Starlings. The nine readers were superb, and essa's performance blew my mind. The poems were powerful and poignant. essa was clearly a poet to watch.

**From 2015 onwards, we were seeing your poems very frequently in online publications and in a lot of magazines. Were you making a concerted effort to put your poetry out into the world from that time, or have you always felt the drive to share and publish?**
Before 2014 I had never even thought about sending poetry to places. I wrote all the time, but just didn't consider publishing anything, except for on Tumblr.

**So was this new drive for publication to a particular end?**
I took these creative writing papers at the University of Waikato under Tracey Slaughter, and she was hugely supportive of my writing. She said, 'You've got to send your stuff out.' I just listened to her and rode on her enthusiasm. It became its own thing, then — a habit. To get your work

recognised by editors of journals who are supposed to know what is good and what isn't was nice. It was also rewarding to put something that's usually very private into the world. I think there are a lot of things that tell you that your voice isn't important or is superfluous, or maybe what you have to say is frivolous, and so it's good to have it validated.

**And you had a name change in 2017. There were reasons for that obviously not connected with poetry, but did your work being published have anything to do with it?**
A lot of things kind of happened. It started out there was a character in a long poem I wrote for a paper at Waikato called essa. It was a piece exploring the baggage of having my name and exploring gender — who I really wanted to be. And then when I applied to do the MA at IIML (the MA at Waikato wasn't ready at that time), there was a question on the enrolment form asking for your 'preferred name', so I just put 'essa'. I think I'd already told some close friends that they could call me that if they wanted, but that was the first time I'd actually decided that was who I wanted to be. Because I'd moved to a new place, I could be who I wanted to be. Then everyone on the course called me essa because that was what was on the form.

In the middle of that year, I figured out what I wanted my whole name to be. I wanted to keep the essence of what my parents had called me (the meaning was very important to my mum), so 'essa' has the same meaning as my given name ('God-saved'). May is my nan's middle name, and my surname is just the Māori transliteration of Ransfield, my father's English surname. My dad's side is the Māori side of the family.

**Many of your poems are deeply anchored in Māori tradition. However, their personae often come from a perspective of disenfranchisement. So, at once, you demonstrate a significant understanding of Māori culture (which appears to have been hard-won) while presenting a speaker who is frequently positioned outside their own culture. Would you talk a little about your own experience of learning about Māoritanga (and te reo Māori), and how this learning relates to your poetry?**

Kia ora! Yeah, I'm currently learning te reo Māori, and as of yet haven't got a firm handle on it, but I've been trying to incorporate more Māori words and concepts into my writing to increase my familiarity, and to show a voice that is learning but still distanced. I was brought up by my Pākehā side of the family, and so I had very little exposure to my Māori roots growing up. I do feel a bit disenfranchised, so I approach that directly in my writing.

**I have read elsewhere that encountering the work of Robert Sullivan, Vaughan Rapatahana and Hinemoana Baker was revelatory for you. Would you mind talking a little about the New Zealand poets who have been formative influences for you, whether in person or on the page?**
Oh wow. Tracey Slaughter, of course — who also writes an amazing short story. Without that course I wouldn't be so committed to poetry as I am. Vaughan Rapatahana's work showed what was possible in terms of formatting and just pushing the language as far as it can go. Hinemoana Baker's w*aha / mouth* is a treasure to me, as well as Robert Sullivan's *Star Waka,* which I think is an incredible achievement and a book we should be talking about more. Māori in space is like the coolest idea! Contemporaries, too, are so inspiring: Nina Powles and Tayi Tibble.

**What is the most important thing your time studying for your MA at Vic taught you about writing?**
That meaning isn't the enemy.

[We fought this one out for something like half an hour. essa added marvellous statements as I tried to claw my way towards an understanding of what they meant. 'If you turn everything to nonsense, you tear down established structures of meaning'; 'Coming to language in a way that we do not usually come to it can be exciting'; 'Meaning isn't an animal to be hunted'. In the end, I decided that I liked the line 'Meaning is not the enemy' for its elliptical and poetic qualities and we went on to the next question.]

**Apart from the 'meaning' thing, what did you take away with you from your time studying and writing?**

That a lot of poems are trying to figure something out. If you already know it, then you don't need to write the poem.

**That's so true. I love that. So what about when you've written the poem? What makes an individual poem feel 'ready' or 'done' to you? How many edits or incarnations might a typical poem have before it is sent off or read aloud in public?**

Usually it has been through a lot of edits, maybe three or four, before it's felt done, but recently a lot of pieces have gone through only one edit/rewrite and then I've sent them. I usually want to read pieces that aren't finished in public to get a feeling for the piece itself, so those are usually lightly edited first drafts unless I'm reading something that has been published.

**Claudia Rankine said: 'There's no private world that doesn't include the dynamics of my political and social world.'[1] It seems to me that you approach your writing very much like this; the political is never far away from the personal, and, although there is no sense of the reader being told what to think or how to think about an issue, by the end of the poem our emotions have been so thoroughly engaged by the persona that the poem's message cannot help but come through extremely movingly. Do you consider yourself to be a political poet, and do you believe that speaking about political malfeasance is the realm and responsibility of the writer?**

I am a political poet and I think it's everyone's responsibility to engage with politics, this of course includes the writer. Though political art can look like a lot of things, I fear its activist potential is pretty useless disconnected from any specific movement.

**Areas of political science that relate to the body, gender and identity are prevalent in your poems. To what extent do you find poetry to be a**

---

1   Claudia Rankine, 'The Art of Poetry', *Paris Review* 219 (Winter 2016): 141.

**fitting vehicle for the expression of what are fluid and complex states that relate so clearly to power and society?**

I find the poem to be the place where language can be deprogrammed, and so it is super useful in representing interstitial/marginalised experience. I admire work like Cody-Rose Clevidence's *Beast Feast* (2014, Ahsahta Press) and *feeld* by Jos Charles (2018, Milkweed) — also Aaron Apps's *Dear Herculine* (2014, Ahsahta). That last one is in letter form, with the poet writing to Herculine Barbin, whose suicide, in the nineteenth century, was obviously linked to the gender reassignment forced on them by law. It interweaves Apps's experiences with Herculine's. In *ransack*, I have letters to Woolf's Orlando, so I like this idea of the epistolary form a lot, obviously.

**Having published *ransack* now, what is your next project?**

I have so many 'next' projects. I'm obsessed with the epic poem and want to do something in that vein. (The reason I got into reading poetry was *Paradise Lost* by Milton.) I have done so many collaborative pieces and want to do more. I have three manuscripts that have been complete for some time, all focusing on slightly different things. One is like a diary of experimental poetry that engages almost exclusively with my relationship with gender and the body — it functions as a long poem or many short poems. Another manuscript dwells on place and identity a bit more, with the tentative title *homesick*. The third manuscript focuses on Echidna, and it is this kind of mythography that draws on my experiences and fits in to all sorts of traditions, from Classical Greek to Māori oral tradition, to commentary on the global climate disaster. Though I'm unsure of whether these manuscripts will stay separate or be cannibalised into one single mega collection, kind of like Voltron or something.

**It is very possible to imagine essa developing a 'mega collection, kind of like Voltron'. In fact, it is eminently possible to imagine essa doing all sorts of innovative and incredible things in the poetry world. They have the original style and voice that catch attention, and the subject matter that needs attention. If I were a betting woman, I would say put your money here.**

## Select bibliography

**POETRY**
*ransack* (Wellington: Victoria University Press, 2019)

**ZINES**
*daisy bell he sings for bowman* (self-published, 2017)
*if we grew up* (self-published, 2017)
*the bleed screw* (self-published, 2017)
*waka sunk* (self-published, 2018)

**JOURNALS**
*Mayhem* 1 & 2 (2014)
*Cadaverine* (2015)
*Mayhem* 3 (2015)
*The Fem* (2015)
*brief* 55 (2016)
*Mayhem* 4 (2016)
*Geometry* 1 (2017)
*Mayhem* 5 (2017)
*Poetry New Zealand Yearbook 2017*
*Starling* 4 (2017)
*Them* 3 (2017)
*Aotearotica* 6 (2018)
*brief* 56 (2018)
*Landfall* 236 (2018)
*Mayhem* 6 (2018)
*Mimicry* 4 (2018)
*Oscen* (2018)
*Otoliths* (2018)
*Poetry Magazine* (February 2018)
*Poetry New Zealand Yearbook 2018*
*Ruru Reads* (2018)
*Scum Mag* (2018)

*Sport* 46 (2018)
*Starling* 5 & 6 (2018)
*Swamp* 21 (2018)
*takahē* 94 (2018)
*Turbine | Kapohau* (2018)
*Palimpsest* (2019)

**ONLINE**
www.essawrites.wordpress.com

# New
# Poems

# Into the
water

## into the water

when I was six I watched my father
emerge from the sea
carrying flippers
and his face mask

the rubber suit and the oxygen tank
bulked my imagination of sea creatures
as he slowly peeled the skins
and appendages off

I thought my father longed to disappear
from this world

but he always came back
with his sea camera and canisters of film
with images of kelp vistas
and coral cities
with squids, clownfish, and jellies

I swore the next time he changed
into his wetsuit
with its straps and fins and metal lungs
I'd be prepared
with my own skins

and I'd walk backward with him
into the water

John Allison

## Why we fish

*for Mike Allison, d. 28 October 2018*

Those long evenings, flicking
dry flies, nymphs, trying anything to coax
a wily, insolent brown trout
to deviate from its lakeshore beat
and suck it up, strike, sink
down to the bottom, doggo as a snag —
or else to be smashed by
the impetuous rush of a rainbow, never
delicate in its fierce arc.

This is a long-past story for me
foresworn upon my best friend's death, now
given over to my reverie —
meanwhile you became a master
of the form, slipping out when we visited
to fetch a rainbow or a brown
(or did you get it from the freezer?
with your humour we would never know
for sure. I thought it fresh).

Trout fishing is the story of your hope
for what might come —
it is about what you catch, but also always
it is what you think about
when you cast a line towards those shadows
from which solace may be drawn . . .

You know, Mike, I cannot look
at clear water now without thinking of you . . .
Maybe it's time to start again
fetch my fly rod, head off to the river —
to look for you, brother mine,
out on the water at the evening rise.

## The absurdity of fleeing

It was an imperfect plan, my father admits
to ask god to teach him to swim
as he boarded an unreliable boat

and though he didn't drown, others did
who bob face-down in the neck of the gulf

If the oracle had any sense, she would have told him
there's really nothing beyond the border

but you don't know until you know, my father says
In Sana'a he saw an old black man

in the battered street just before curfew hour
his blue-rimmed eyes tired under thick brow

My father scanned his surroundings and asked quietly
*Uncle, are you Somali?*
He replied, *That's the story my mother told me.*

## Boat children

know that windows are sometimes below the waterline
and that Greek porters open and close

the cabin doors in a fluid khoros
we wonder where they go to feed

and why the sound of bouzoukia
is seeping in around the sealed portholes

we wonder if music can drown us and if the porters
are mermen granted legs during the day

## cut by water

sliced to the bone
blood squirming in streams
from a disbelieving wound
whiteshock of exposure
pressure revealing
the fabric of my flesh

such a betrayal, that water
whose caresses only have I known
cushion of descent,
salve of valley floors,
the morning kiss of mist
that holds you in the bed
a minute more

water, never more threat
than chill mountain nip
on morning's toes
& still prepared to carry
your sins downstream, water
that until this moment
has parted as you pass

recount the rivers of your past
trusted guides & fair
that claimed your sweat
& tears as kin,
that carried your secrets
untold to the sea,
consort & comforter

all this, yet sudden
she lays me open.
I am undone

Bryan Walpert

## In the lull

now, after the heavy rain — the kind
whose sudden arrival, whose shocking
weight, even if forecast, sends anything
alive scurrying for cover without care
for dignity — when it is still
possible to hear the water sluice
along drainpipes, through gutters,
along any slanted surface, he watches it
puddle in the grass he would cut as she
watched him through that same window
from the house on a hill whose lawns
rise now unimpeded like any perverted
vision of freedom: an absence
she made clear always clouded
the horizon, weather whose arrival,
more so for being forestalled,
haunted every blooming pōhutukawa,
each bloody magnolia,
only these words a final
awkward rushing after,
water whispering a memory
of what it once was even as it ebbs
by following in reverse the road
they'd climb to get home each day,
their mouths dry from the effort
of its long, implacable gradient.

John Howell

## Shibboleth

At a narrow ledge of stony beach
in a pocket of calm between sharp rocks
we shelter our grief.

Within the sea's rips and undercurrents,
deceptively flat like our faces,
our eyes search for words of love.

We surge and drain like the tide,
embrace the salt air,
find each other again.

Jeni Curtis

## talking of goldfish

they say a goldfish remembers
nothing   doomed to endless circles
of a bowl   the waterweed waving
in a familiar kind of way
like a memory    that lurks
just around the corner

who knows what a flounder
thinks of    the flatness
of the estuary might lend
credence to the flatness of the earth
the rise and ebb of tides   repetition
and cycles of comforting predictability

salmon too are given
to recollection   how to read
the signs of the shingled river mouth
which stream to follow   the instinctual
leap of faith over slick glazed rocks
light catching water in sudden radiance

herrings bow to Jung   a collective
unconscious   in flurried shoals
too numerous to count   the silver circling
of a single thought   not caught
in the individual moment but
a massed dream of blue and darkness

and I remember you   moments
like droplets that gather into water
gush and rush into streams
into lakes   a sea of memory
in which I swim   I sink   I drown

bring back your boat   your net
and catch me

## Six offices of a monk seal

*i vigils*
Pre-dawn glows in her iris
mouth open like a bell
she expels pebbles
and chants with swells

*ii prime*
She plucks tufts of silver-grey
fur from rock pools
and weaves a mute seal pup

*iii midday prayer*
The hour of ocean psalms
and diving through shoals of fish

*iv terce*
howl of storms
surge of pups
hunger of caves

*v vespers*
On the thin edge of the ocean
dogs of the sea run in rough water

*vi compline*
Into her mouth
she returns a pebble
for the scars of mating

a pebble
for beach lactation

a pebble
for genetic variability

a pebble
for the great silence
that lasts until dawn

## The Reef, Mangaia

When Papatua walks from Kaumata to the reef at dusk,
south of the rā'ui, and waist deep through warm lagoon waters,
he wears purple running shoes and his green Turtles singlet
In one hand he carries the surf caster he bought in Sydney
A kitchen knife in the other, in case of clams

And there, coming in slow from her time on the reef,
is Mama No'o. Thigh-deep in the low tide, with kikau fish basket
and screwdriver. A red t-shirt, and pāreu around her waist
She is shucking pāua, eating as she walks

Red reef fish — kū — fried whole. Rūkau vītī steamed, with kuru
in coconut cream. You pull the fish apart with your fingers
Pick it bare to its sweet, white bones. Papatua leans over,
takes your fish in his hands and sucks at its head. The eyes
and the brains are best, he says

And again later, after midnight. A new moon scratching
the horizon, Papatua is back wading towards the ocean's edge
This time with his underwater torch, a plastic sack
tied to his back, and the gardening gloves he uses
to prise crayfish from their coral clefts. If the tide is right,
he says, they will be ascending
    – coming up to a bowl of fizzing starlight

Before dawn the sky is butter melting on toasted bread
The lagoon is a silver-handled knife held still and tight
    – knuckles of coral

The reef, its sharp blade, pares back the skin
of another day. And there is blood,
    – and it is falling into the ocean.

## Logbook

How much is remembered —
even on a ferry
crossing the harbour

\*

The inland frown
of a boy
from a farm.

\*

Like ancient epics
foreign ships
flying the flags of great lines.

\*

How much is forgotten —
even on a ferry
returning from an island

\*

Astern
vineyards and wakes
intertwine.

On a hill above the sea
the wind is turning
dark blue pages —

the logbook of pine trees.

## The Literary Coast

This poem is yet another shot
at the message I've been trying
to write for years then seal inside
a bottle and cast into the waves,
begging to be rescued —

or if (as seems more likely)
deliverance is impossible
at least to provide a desperate
warning to the last true versifiers
not to set sail blithely

for the Literary Coast
without fortitude, plenty of grog,
a thick dictionary, a mattress
and an umbrella. As I squat here
shipwrecked on a reef

picking shellfish off the rocks
I am sustained only by a faith
in meaningless directions
a pleasure in popping words
like seaweed pods and a hope

that my protection won't blow
inside out. Which isn't much
when set against home comforts
but it's been enough to take
the place of better things —

especially when I add to it
the delicious company
of mermaids singing as they comb
their flowing tresses. One in particular
really gets me going.

Elizabeth Nannestad

## Rain

It is raining.
People complain about it.
Who are these people? Don't they feel
sad sometimes? Weren't they
held, well-loved, when they were small?
Rain touches you and asks for nothing.
It is bigger than you.
You had so many things to do, lists of them, and the rain came and
took half of them away and the rest just stay there, stay there, quiet
for once, not even adding to themselves, stay there looking back at
you like 'now what?' but meaning nothing, not a single thing. And
fading.

When it comes it seems it will always be here.
From a great distance you can watch it moving, sweeping, queenly,
across the sea, across the land, gathering mountains.
It is fair.
And afterwards, there will be peace in the grass.
And though by any measure the rain is vast, so that you can't see the
beginning or the end of it, you look out your window into the rain
and in your mind you hold it in one hand, entirely, a misty ball,
crystalline, shockingly fresh and cool, an exact fit for your palm,
holding it and rolling it around a little, you breathe on it and stir
your finger on it for the pleasure of it, and then it's you that is vast,
grown tall and light in every direction, fearless, the comforter of all.
Such is the rain.

Such are we, in the rain,
not even dizzy from swapping sizes with the universe but not
admitting it either. Not telling anyone.
And neither will we say
what we find
inside it when we go there,

letting ourselves in.

Only we stand at the window looking out and forget about other things.

When we do turn from the window the first thing we see

destroys us with love, so that we stumble, a failure of a father towards
the child he lost, cast off, bewildered, sticky with tears, adam's apple
sharp and hurting inside, wet, pathetic and overcome, reaching
out — all the Christmases, all the birthdays, gone! All your faults fly
up at once, a swarm of them, pestilential. And will she allow him to
come any closer? No! No! No she will not. She is unaware. Reaching
out, deeply sorrowful and admiring —

but the first thing we see
is not that child
but another thing, although let's say
it is the child, you found her, on her birthday.

You went blank for a moment. No one noticed. It passed
apart from a memory
of standing
fragile
on your own
heart necessarily broken, everything broken and left out to get rained
on.

Someone was there with you,
but you have forgotten.

Someone smiled because of you, and this you have almost but not
completely forgotten.

Someone was present, for you — yes: a *presence*, and look — there
are old metro tickets in your pocket, you must have gone through
turnstiles but now you have no recollection, even what country
you were in or why so one thing you know is, it is a long way back
and would take a lot of detection, you could try the sewing box, the

box you were given but never used for sewing but to keep things in, things, like a stone — but where have you put it, that box? It has a silk lining, quilted. Surely you didn't throw it out? No! you'd keep it, surely — — — but by now whoever that was has gone, into the crowd, underground, or home address unknown, clicking the front gate to the garden, leaving you behind. So you decide to leave them too, because you feel you have to. It was a woman.

A coat, a good raincoat, is what you want but then what about being wet, all wet, when magically nothing is 'wet' anymore? You have missed that, haven't you? Having a wet, wet tummy.
Even if you buy a good coat, you might not have it with you. Even if you do have it with you, one day the rain finds a way in, a hole you didn't know about, in one shoe, sneaks in and reminds you — of you.

It has no name although we call it *rain*,
and no words, only an impression it gives
which stays a short time
a very short time
afterwards.

## Experiments Touching Cold (3)

We often use the word freeze
in the transitive sense
to signify the operation
upon other bodies,
is what I was thinking,
or, rather, abruptly recollecting
from my reading, as it had started
to hail, so I missed the last thing
she said, and to cover that lapse
I slid open the glass door
of the deck to hear the patter
against the boards, the softer
ticking against the trees,
the worrisome tinnier clatter
on the roofs of cars, ours,
having left them on the drive,
and because we had been talking
for what must have been two hours
when the hail started to fall,
covering and recovering ground,
like a word repeated over and over
the sense of things was becoming lost,
leaving only a general memory that
there was a sense behind it, a terrain
we had long mapped in our heads,
each of us starting with the position
that the other had inflicted some
measure of damage, though
perhaps less certain now,
as it had grown quite late,
of course, the conversation
growing more strident,

as the ice fell faster,
pummelling the cars,
reaching a sort of intensity
that had us now in a surprising communion
before the window, knowing
it would be clearer in the morning
when in a more sympathetic light,
perhaps after some sleep,
we would be better
positioned to stand back to assess
what might at some cost be repaired,
what we might live with.

Alison Denham

## Iron Bridge, Buller Gorge

The iron bridge works loose a board from one lane, a tongue . . .
And suddenly everything speaks at once . . .

Too much heavy iron gripes the river bank
alive with fern fringed eyes.

Beneath the bridge water chants and gurgles
around the milestones, the beautiful rough boulders . . .

Be glad we never dammed after the earthquake of '29,
but found a way to seep through the new rock fall.
We live it still, the punts, the floods, your horses shiny with fear,
old hotels we flow past, taken by fire.

You crossed over here many times,
time replays and sound loops back, the last
stands of bush hammered and cursed, shingle
and quartz gravel razzle in the pans.

Long before you found the next valuable thing we'd
gone on ahead into the past.

## Two Waters

All winter the rain blubs on the shoulder of Ihumātao.
The main drag splutters under people's gumboots.

Children squeal and catch raindrops on their tongues
in the place where the cat got the tongue of their ancestors.

Everything is going on. Laugh and cry and yin and yang,
kapu tī and singing in the white plastic whare.

On the perimeter people hold hands in a tukutuku pattern.

The plans of the developers hologram over the lush grass.

Day and night, police cars cluster like union jacks —
red white and blue, and oblique, and birds fly up.

A hīkoi carries the wairua across the grey city.
Auckland Council can take a hike. It's the wettest winter.

The signatures of the petition sprout from the two waters.

The sky falls into the earth, the earth opens its memory.

# Encounter

Michael Hall

## Encounter

On a day
Not much different
From this one,
I will chance
Upon an old man.

He and I
Will sit
Side by side
By the window
At the same table

Confused with sunlight.
Have we learnt nothing
You and I?
Drink your tea,
Old man, I'll say —

Fardowsa Mohamed

## Tuesday

the sun through the kitchen windows carpeted the tiles
like orange prayer mats and my mother was singing the folk song
I had memorised without understanding. steam rose from the stove
and condensed on the discoloured ceiling as she baked canjeero.
I ate five to impress my father, who told me to eat so that you are strong,
eat to feed your power. and I believed him, even if just for the morning
before the world rose against me. my mother hurried me into the car
as I nervously tugged at my strange clothes, picking out the ugly
before others did it for me. she held my chin up with her thumb and said:
*It is only Tuesday, macaanto. The week is young and the days have not
yet worn her down.*

## White Noise

In the way of genetics
my white body with my white husband's
has made a beautiful son
whose features mean when he's alone with me
he's been taken as part Samoan;
or a scion maybe of Jamaican ancestry.
The guesswork comes in every size
from idle curiosity to sneers street-side:

> *Hey, Afro Man! Where's y' daddy gone?*
> *Hey, Barak O'Pākehā! Where you think you're from?*

We've always walked past it
as so much white noise:
as if to ignore ignorance
might make any bigot
a better, bigger man.

Yet the day I hear an ex-cop
in a holiday park trailer
has told our son his curly hair and facial bones
should help him get ahead with jazz musos
*''cause blacks and islanders have natural rhythm,'*

the car that spitfires past us
mimics the bullet-whine of injustice
and for a riven moment
my blood is terror's ice mirror
for the mother who knows

how little time there is to drill her child in —

*Do not under any circumstances*

say 'Please just leave me alone' to a police officer

sell CDs on the street and thereby come to the attention of a police officer

ask why you have to put out your cigarette in your own car when told to by a police officer

be homeless, have a history of addiction, or mental health issues in the vicinity of a police officer

have cardiac, lung or weight problems when dealing with a police officer


pull your arm away from a police officer

be wheelchair-bound and try to adjust your seated position if approached by at least 3 police officers

*Sweet-son, at all times, when approached by cops, you must*

Drop your sunglasses, drop your cellphone.
Drop your textbooks, your hickory drum-sticks.
Drop your house-keys, drop your sandwich.
Drop your wallet, drop your camera.

Show both hands emptied and bare.
Fly both palms' pale flags of surrender.

## Rock Art

The sign said Maori Rock Drawings
so no wonder the mature male cyclist
said to the group of women
what makes the pigeons Māori?
He cackled at his own joke.
I allowed it to ruin my drive
to Omārama — I nearly turned
around to talk to him,
but then allowed the land,
the other limestone cliffs
with our tupuna art,
our taonga tuku iho,
remind me what was what
and who was who.

## Māori is my Name:
## A poem for my father.

I feel like I'm dying.
Sharp pains in my chest,
While they spit in my face.
I'm holding, keeping, saving,
Cherishing my breath.
     Because they're not speaking for me
     Or even speaking to me —
     They are speaking at me
     In brackish sprays of jumbled words, spit out
Loud and hoarse from an old crusted mouth
Whose dementia of reality is so compromised
That they have made up their own version of history
And their own language by which to explain it.
     And with these headlines they assault me,
As if their gibberish is a lethal weapon
  Against my body
Of factual, documented, historical knowledge.

     Withstand and infiltrate, like a timed grenade.
Because how deeply their ignorance wounds me and
Wounds the child self, which
Otherwise holds them dearly,
Not knowing where else to turn to for instruction
On how to survive
These hunger games.
     Looking for answers in every direction but my own,
Blinded by the false beauty
Of shiny plastic crowns.

     Released is that wrinkly ugly hand.
I am holding my own wrist,
Practising First Aid,

I've got fingertips pressed to the pulse
Counting the beats at rest.
        From this beat, beat, beat I can tell
That the only health issue I have ever had
Was believing *their* lies
And making their sickness
*Mine.*

        I tried to change my skin colour
To match their 50 shades of grey court room wigs.
        I hated *myself*
        Because of their lies.

        I had to forgive myself
        For ever believing their lies
And now I love myself for seeing their lies.

Because I know that I was only ever trying to change someone's mind.
Both theirs and simultaneously . . . Mine . . .
        Trying to change the being
        Instead of being the change
To make this world a better place.

        And in that way
I was wasting precious time. Because
Almost every attempt at constructive, collective, creative diplomacy
Fell apart at the seams
        Like the urine-soaked, potato-sack dress
        Of a little brown girl who didn't know how
        To gibberish for the bathroom
And found herself strapped and caned for trying to leave the classroom.
        Like a village of women, children and elders
        Who had prayerfully taken pages of Holiness
        Through native eyes to native skin —

Like paper armour for the soul —
But were marched upon and burned alive
On the pews of a Christian church.

So no wonder,
Now in the middle of all the compromises
We are stalking the ground, enraged
Birthing a raped pregnancy
That bears only half the fruits of our labour.
We are biting at the bits
For in the process of compromise
We are faced and demeaned by
Rotten pips of influential ego
And the poor craftsmanship of our
So-called 'Democracy'.

Because, let's face it, not one of us is
Quite the carpenter that Jesus was:
The divide-and-conquer sacred Son.
But I know ... The demigod Māui,
Stopped that very sun
In its path across the sky,
Just as I stop this union jack
In separating blood from blue and white.

Because like Māui, I know the truth
That one needs more than just a little ray of sunlight
To warm the face,
One needs more than the indigenous version
Of our national anthem
Playing daily on the air waves
To heal these ears
That are so betrayed

After all the years of
Comments about those cheeky Ds . . .
Those happy little Vegemites . . .
Proper nouns pronounced incorrectly . . .
Committed to song and slogan
And sung to us like lullabies.
We need more than a single line in a dictionary to define
Tūrangawaewae.
More than a flapping flag
To show
The depth
Of
Our
Tino
Rangatiratanga.
I need more than just foreign friends
To understand that apartheid means apartheid.

     Some achievements have been won with bravery, but
I need more to be happy.
     I am not content with winning a spit fight
Or even stirred by the deflection
Of salt water to the eye.
     I require more than a huge dose of cultural sedatives,
That can only be administered in the lessons
Of a language which should already be my own
     But instead is taught to me within the walls
Of a second, third, fourth, fifth home —
A series of upliftings to take us down a peg.
     Come, Gen X, Y and Z,
Suck the marrow from the bones
Of our tipuna long past.

I believe that they would agree
With a modern form of cannibalee,
A devouring of knowledge like it is a laxative
To relieve a spiritual constipation,
An anal tension that has been caused
By too many boots to the arse
From a so-called equal judiciary system that only
Promotes privatised suicide and
Statistical over-representation.

Because while my pulse is not stable at rest,
    I am
Twisted in my guts and blue around the mouth,
Starving in the plastic world.
I will let this life-form die a thousand deaths
And martyr myself just for us all to abandon
    Their abusive plan

And let a waking sleep guide me to
A dream that is also real,
A dream
Of a journey home
Down a long, not-often-trodden dirt road
To a one-hundred-year old house
Nestled in unconfiscated hills,
Its cloak-like wallpaper
And precious wooden photo frames,
Its smell of love and forever.
A farmhouse with falling piles
And holes in the concrete kitchen floor,
Where the slugs crawl in at night time
And listen to our stories.
Because here is where my father was born

And here is where he knew
That there is so much more to knowing
And boldly carrying our wounds.

'The name gives its tapu
To that which bears its name.'

And my name is Māori.

John Allison

## Crows (slightly gothic) in Croydon

They're a jagged black hole
light disappears into, re-emerging only
as their dismal call:
*narc ... nah ... naa-aarc ... !*

The sort of noise the world might make
if you could crowbar
open any of its aching surfaces
and let out its primal cry

this mouthing of such bleak utterances
at passer-by pedestrians.
Bad black jokes
flapping down pole to pavement

yet no one really notices the crows
encroaching on the nerves
of Croydon, scraping
pain from the loosened edges of the mind.

Behind the locked loo block
out the back a homeless man needles
embroidered veins
and staggers off through the gate

into those van Gogh
cornfields the crows continue to inhabit ...
Though with dusk
even they fall silent, disappearing

in the cracks of darkness
spreading all along the elm's branches.
The gate forecloses
on any further possibilities.

## Ghost poem #1 — Exciting new trends in necromancy

I talk to ghosts and unfortunately they talk back with unsolicited advice on how to get my séance body ready in time for Halloween. They tell me what's trending. Common ghosts. Foreign ghosts. Ghosts with unfinished business lurking in the basement wearing their best silent treatment. Ghosts sent to me like flat-pack furniture delivered without an instruction manual, just an 0800 number direct dial to the dead. What is this part for and how does it fit together? Who designed this and am I missing something? But the helpline is automated and it doesn't understand my accent, so I compose strongly worded tweets asking for free stuff. Old-timey white sheet ghosts. If eyes are the windows to the soul please explain two holes in a white sheet. Ghost of calling in sick on Mondays. Ghost of 'Please check your balance'. Ghost of calls coming from inside the house. Who knew that a ringtone could announce a ghost!? That the disembodied voice on the other end is more conversational than murder-y bringing new pathos to otherwise overdone expectations of where the plot might be headed — a parody to answer the vibrations around us, like Coldplay's 'Yellow' but replace each instance of 'yellow' with 'YOLO'. A ghost in the audience ready to dispute the 'we only have one life' argument. A ghost has a life! A ghost has hopes and dreams! Ghosts in search of a redemption edit — as in X — as in 'lost feeling from the scalp down but still a hero in some people's eyes'. Again with the eyes! Again with the white sheets, a modern-day example of spectral oppression. We should be outraged on their behalf. We should enforce a ban on the white sheet for security and freedom! A stumble of ghosts disappearing into my overactive imagination granting no wishes or glimpses into the future but simply escorting me to corners that will keep me quiet. A surprise ending. A ghost with no answers, just a reason to hang around until someone turns the lights on.

# Ghost poem #2 — Identity crises

The first ghost is your contingency plan —
a packed suitcase hidden in the wardrobe
a stolen identity plucked from an old phone book
your memory trained to instantly recall
the names and addresses of people you can trust
when you arrive in your shades and newly bleached hair
with a soft English accent that won't arouse suspicion.
This ghost told you the revolution would be over
before the sceptics had a chance to file their stories.
You fix yourself in crowds and survey the entrances
and exits of the people around you, careful not
to make eye contact with anyone. You were once
tested, your loyalty workshopped by a room of spooks.
This ghost let you walk out of conflicts without
entering them in the first place.


~


The second ghost is your shield in crossfire
stripping the danger from the inevitable unknown.
These days, all your fairy tales end in divorce
so this ghost makes sure you are ready to respond
in the most appropriate manner — floating
with the rest of us in a sea of modern apathy.
Even when a newsreader announces the unthinkable
with a crack in their voice that betrays their own shield
ignore that swelling in your chest to
abandon ship                abandon words
and turn your attention to the ghosts we willingly let go
or the ghosts we lead to water because we can't bear
to speak their names any longer. Nostalgia is so passé.
Let's sing the end of the world into being.

~

The third ghost's fists are filled with opinions
beating on every front door in the quiet hours
until someone welcomes him inside to lie down
on their couch so he can ask why — why is there misery/
why is no one listening/why won't the birds stop
screaming when their wings are torn off?
I know now that when I loved this ghost
in another life          he unmade me
as I now unmake him to map him across a terrain
neither of us are willing to cross. He had
many questions then too and I had no answers
fit for his purposes. I am deeply sorry
and deeply remorseful.
I have not taken the time to forget this ghost.


~

The fourth ghost — an admission of true death — the one
who turned away from hope and the benefits of believing
in hope — stands at the edge of the precipice
and calls out to me in his usual game. I am there
on the horizon — smoke as a flock of birds
abandoning seasons. I am only as fast as the storm
behind me and as sure as the land
that settles beneath my feet. I taunt this ghost.
This ghost retaliates. And so on, and so on.
We have come so far we no longer remember
who made the first move, who said the first words
and who has the courage to shut down the night.

Rosetta Allan

## Opening night with Dracula

*St Petersburg, Russia*

His name was Tame, he said, though he didn't hold out his hand for
  me to shake.

He appeared in the middle of a room brimming with humans
electrified on wine and creative banter, then broke through three knots
of closely guarded huddles before entering the proximity of me —
that private space pried open on these first nights —
the flesh and bone me who prefers not to be seen
deflects the gaze anywhere else
but most especially toward that other me
the one hung by hooks and string
sanctified by the white of gallery walls
secure inside wooden frames
untouched behind glass casing.

His name was Tame, he said, and the name hung suspended between us.

I am Russian Maori, he said, which explained the sternness of his stare,
the blackness of his eyes packed tight with old ghosts.
I calculated the black curls of his hair. He stooped his head
gently forward shoulders hunched in apology for his height.
Two large paintings rose up either side of him —
wings of Pounamu green as if that's what they had always intended to be.
My mother is from New Zealand, he said, and I wanted to see his hands —
those skinny limbs stuffed inside black leather pockets.
And your father, I asked, he was a vampire?
Tame smiled, a human smile, and in it I saw his mother.

Later that night, I roll my blinds all the way open.
Let the defuse light of the white night illuminate my skin.
I calculate the moon.
I wonder if he could climb the walls to my window
from the courtyard below — sink his fingernails

into the weather-beaten concrete as though it were sand.
I wonder if he would fly and transform before me if I open my windows to the cold of the night. Or if he would come through the black entrance, climb the haggard ribs of the tired old back stairs if I unlock the metal door.

His name was Tame, I say, but the night is too calm for vampires.

## 6 Laburnham Street

Enter. Please enter. Step over the meat patty stamped into the path. Ignore the cigarette butts; they are not carpet. Knock on the door. It will always be opened. Look at the man who lives here; the one with the entire ocean in his eyes. Don't be frightened if he calls you a bitch. Try not to worry if he tells you that he is being: poisoned, hunted, murdered, or confesses his virginity. Stay for a while. Sit on the worn couch and take him in your arms. For as long as he'll let you. For as long as you can hold on. After the embrace, make a cup of tea. Notice the passion fruit vine growing near the kitchen window; he planted that. And if you wait quietly beside him you'll see he hears the plant's song.

### the light in hotels looks forward to welcoming you again soon

The light in hotels is a hymn to the posture of a woman half-used
in an oil-painting, the colour of memory sipped from an eat-in
menu of polystyrene choices.
The light in hotels is a tabernacle of collarbones.
The light in hotels is wearing a fixture of flies preheated to a two AM
sonnet.
The light in hotels wants to unbutton everything, a long false kiss at
the crosshairs of your sternum.
It is not alabaster. It will sing like a swingdoor of lovers on all fours,
oh the honeying.
The light in hotels is against you spread-eagled in the cheap
luminosity of innermost sitcoms.
The moulted bedspread lies spotlit for a late night rubbing of
unpalatable truths.
It holds mosquitos on a leash in its inhuman solitude.
The light in hotels reassembles his gasp at the mirror where your pale
thighs scalp him.
Wipeclean, the light in hotels leaves you buzzcut.
On all quiz shows the last answer is: thou shalt covet the light in
hotels.
The light in hotels is a summons to dye your hair so he can lace up
your headwounds.
Seek & you shall find the recommended brace position in the light of
hotels.
Queue at reception for a sleeve of small crimes you can perform in
the skull of the lampshade, a four legged SOS, your wedding ring off
the hook.
The light in hotels is what you're saddled with.
It will lead you to the vertigo of teacups & sachets of single-serve
anti-matter.

The light in hotels is a legacy of eyeshadow, each tear weighing a
tinted ounce.
The light in hotels can lip-read the *fuck-mes* uttered at the back of
your mind. It has no gravitas.
The light in hotels degenders the stains on the bed with the scent of
parted legs, but the quaver of a child caught in a distant hallway.
It will issue you emergency instructions to dream.
Be silent in the light of hotels.
It's reflected from the nearby neon hospital of non-invasive love.
It's a glass disc of apostrophes, a crown of disintegrated moths, soft
lint of short-circuited thoraxes.
It forgets where you parked the black accident of your courtesy car.
(Did you think this was a getaway?)
It tastes like a relic of hair on the showerdoor, a shampooed
genuflection.
It will always sin with you. It makes every girl an island.
Book now to tour your next abasement in the three-and-a-half-star
light of hotels.
It's a catalogue of burnt nerve endings.
It is ending.
Arise and blame the light in hotels.
It remembers your freckles, their exact leopardprint.
Stand on this X where you cannot change your spots.

## Swerve

She descends the long, wet track
walled on one side by a moss-draped cliff,
giving on the other into blackberry tangle,
dark fern, abrupt marine-blue trench of empty air.
As the children pelt ahead, voices high coppery bells,
their light, tousled brows bobbing like colts',
memory suddenly veers

to that café corner, a friend
at the too-small, awkward table,
his fingers as careful on the menu
as if a hidden blade might slip;
words poised, as if the truth he sought
called for the same delicate probe
of tongue tip sensing tiny, splintered bones.

There, right then:
another vertiginous brink;
something dear skated too near an edge
in his cautious talk,
even before the alarm on his face,
hands flown to his skull as if he were the one
bowled over on the crossing outside —

God, the hot shriek of brakes, sick metal scrape,
the sliding, barrelling, as a motorbike spun on its flank,
a young bystander skittled, sprawled,
who surely too soon
staggered up from the tarmac,
to dust off his coat, shake away aid,
give the appalled crowd a curt wave;

the motorcyclist, too, bizarrely unharmed,
yet agog at that traffic Lazarus:
his own hands abrupt, dashing tears
from his snatched-off helmet
as if they were the hot-fat sizzles
of aggravated wasps . . .

time jumbled, chaotic light-warp of collision —
saffron thorns of sun, snapdragon mouths,
scent of cloves, slender throat, tiny spurs
of grass, hair, glass, the fishbowl of the very air;
a fact's fearsome weight crushed along the ribs
as if some vital structure were collapsing;

the man, then, opposite her, startled
into intimate confession:
desire's rapid swerve
as if already his mind, in trauma,
were compelled to repeat
the hurtle, the fearful skid;
the vivid, living minute
the palimpsest of its history
all risked at the limits of her skin.

C. K. Stead

## An encounter in Belsize Park Gardens

Grey hair, grey suit, blue tie, and on the lapel
a huge green brooch — this passing Indian asks
'Sir, Madame, could you spare a moment to talk?'

and the bloodshot eyes are suddenly full of tears.
'Talk . . . of course. Is there something . . . Are you unwell?'
'Thirty-five bloody years I've lived in that flat.'

Eviction? No. He tries to explain his weeping.
'I am not sure I exist. How can I know —
thirty-five years . . .' And again the tears gush forth.

There had been times . . . Just once he'd been in a lab
with Einstein. That was his year in Princeton.
Now he had no colleagues, no wife, no children,

but last night walking on Primrose Hill he'd seen
the marvellous moon's eclipse — a miracle.
His brown face shone through its tears. Today he'd bought

paper and brushes and would paint it. We both
smiled, approving. He asked our names. I said 'Karl,
and this is Minerva.' He told us his

and asked would we please promise to say it
aloud somewhere so he'd know he was alive
outside his own self-knowledge. I said 'Tonight

I'll be in Paris. I'll say your name full voice
in the Marais, and even shout it: "*Albert!*" '
Could that be right? It was the name he'd given.

## Home Video

This is for Donna
on the other side of the world
who does not live here to witness family moments
but reads them like gossip magazines
between the lines written on aerogramme paper
or in packaged videotapes

What do I say?
you ask quite directly
this is for Donna
who is behind the box with its round lens
people eat dip from hollowed bread
small chicken nibbles
peck at half a scone

What do I say?
you ask quite directly
this is for Donna
tell her about school who is your teacher what's your room number
don't be silly as you grin
kick your brother under the little table

What do I say?
you ask quite directly
this is for Donna
watching the static-lined screen

Elizabeth Smither

## Cilla, writing

We are the shortest laureates.\* But this afternoon
Cilla almost touches the sky, writing
on her motel balcony, two storeys up.

Her head in its peaked cap, her pen
are outlined in a strange significant shadow
a little laureate outlined by Rouault

and in the shadows a shorter laureate watching
admiring her application, her skywriting.
The day moon is there, the blinding sun.

Her neck grows warm, her neat head bends
over the page, she stretches her arms
and seems to frown and squint.

It is words, you clowns, the other laureate thinks
not sun in her eyes, not pain of thought
but heart and pen at work again.

---

\*   Cilla McQueen (2009–2011) and Elizabeth Smither (2001–2003) are the two shortest
    poets laureate.

## Decline & Fall

*Hawaii, 2017*

The lexicologist out of his depth
is not waving.

He casts his line
into the ebbing tide — *a clutch*

*of turtle eggs   a silence of cicadas   a convenience*
*of portaloos*

The full moon that broke
a cloak of dappled cloud falls on a comma,

a sleeper under a palm, beside Louis Vuitton
Prada, Rolex, Victoria's Secret.

The dull pewter of sea polished by moonlight,
a climate clement to homelessness.

Dancing with foxes and cougars, the lexicologist
wears the fragrance of wind and night on his shirt.

He avoids the eye of a hungry
dog.

After *aloha*, a *mai tai, mahalo,*
the tongue seizes.

## Station

A cleaner found him on the restroom floor
like something stranded when the tide
went out. She crouched, and knew,
and blessed him on her knees beside
the bucket, closed his stare. She made
the call and waited with him till they came,
stood silent vigil while they raided,
rearranged and stretchered out his form.
She mopped the stalls, scrubbed tiles
and basins, running late but taking care
to wash the restroom of its human spills,
bone-sore, and more than usually aware
of time and needing not to be alone
and needing not to miss the last train home.

Emma Harris

## Ward

On my way to bed late tonight
I looked in on you —
listened to you breathing,
watched your eyelashes flutter
in time with your dreams,
smiled at the way you throw
your limbs wide, like a starfish
whose rockpool has never known threat.

I remembered my childhood sleep,
disturbed by parents
who dropped accusations like
spitfires hurling spite.
Evacuated to Nanna's house,
I would draw the velour curtains tight,
spin the dimmer all the way down
and sit at her feet while she spun stories
about a little girl lost in the woods
who always,
somehow,
found her way home.

She gave my hair one hundred strokes and more
until it crackled with invisible sparks,
flying up to meet the nylon bristles.
She taught me to shell fresh peas,
that blue makes a white wash whiter
and that rubbing a candle on runners
can unstick a stubborn drawer.
She brought me shiny paper from
cigarette packets to fold
into tiny swans that left
the woodiness of tobacco on my fingertips

for as long as I refused to wash them.
Once home, I'd sleep with
my hands tucked beneath my cheek,
holding a head of lavender from her garden,
the mingled scent a ward against hostile whispers
that stormed walls.

Tonight, I checked the flock of origami
birds guarding your windowsill —
ducks, cranes, geese and swans —
while, in the quiet,
a cricket sang on the balcony.

I will take
natural
orders

Peter Clague

## prayer of convalescence

creek hum low
quench my ear

fern drink light
quell my eye

mist breathe soft
salve my skin

I will take natural orders:
  surrender my watch
  shoulder my load
  sling my fears

forest halve me
make me whole

Sarah Penwarden

## Canopies

Stop and listen. Still your body so you are the tuning fork of the world, waiting for the vibration to come. There, in the bushes. Kōkako, kererū, tūī. Stitchbird, bellbird, whitehead. Name them, speak their language of whistles and trills as they chase each other through the trees. Tūī blue black, white lace ruffs and flashes of midnight, swerve and dive, dart and fall. A kererū, rat-red eyes, white front and green wings like a farmer's tan, eats berries with its claw. While up above us one screeches across the high sky. It stalls and falls, falls, falls, then swoops over our heads. Wings edged in silver against a pale sky. What do you call the light from heaven? you ask. And later, I see it in the photo of me, dappled under trees, and the quiet roof of the canopies covering our path.

## **Muriwai, Te Henga, Anawhata, Piha, Karekare**

Haloed by squalls ferny steeps trickle.

Nīkau's green spears shake off drizzle.

Gulls stalk fizz of damp black grains.

Over velvet footprints shallows sidle.

Rollers crash where stingray shades float.

Bubbles wreathe foam's silky prisms.

Bladderwrack tentacles flex their gloss.

Small frogs slide through bush pockets.

Five gannets stitch the sky in single line.

Chris Holdaway

## Albany

Waiting for photographs somewhere
Creation isn't done yet. Narcotic lines in brick
Build an immediately aged face, and the ground
Had to be reduced to clay before it could become
Brown grass & daisies in the wake of
Construction. Halting. Cinder walls left out
In the blitz; village greens whose greatest
Ambition is to be trimmed with violence.
The dried pool,
Beyond how Hadrian left the long fountains
Of his villa, reflecting a fever to rival the sky.
I just wanted to paint houses — think carefully
About the right reed to whet my mouth with
Climbing from water like for the first time. Heat
Carries a wasp away and this year I'm still in love.
Bending to pick a flower; bending through
Tiles & plaster blown across the hill.

## Leaving The Old Slaughterhouse, Hector

*'If you can get out of it, do while there's still time.'*
*Cronshaw* — Of Human Bondage

Our rented ute shudders down from the Slaughterhouse,
arcs a switchback of matted ditch-grass onto the coastal
highway heading south. To the left: king ferns umbrella
from the foothills, nīkau palms pom-pom in the breeze.
Swathes of pigeonwood, flax, rimu, silver beech — all jade
and apple-green. The wet growth glistens, blends in a hum . . .

In certain curves the lowland bush reveals the Tasman Sea —
its breakers at dusk like teeth crushing into a plum. Veins
of cream foam spider out through the limestone — stacks
arched like acrobats frozen mid-play in the shoals. Froth
lavishes the umber clefts, then fizzles out to golden glass —
water gleaming in the same scars it first carved . . .

\*

Last night, held in a den high over the sea, I read by
the bronze flicker of a Franklin stove. Above the Tasman,
one bruisy gash persisted — a sole wound refusing the night-
fall's pink mend. The strobes it faltered on the water told
of discord — moody lights elbowing and spitting with what
breaths might be their last. I stepped onto the balcony, the chitter
and flash of that fire like a mirror set to my geode heart . . .
What mutes the crystal racket of its want?

I went back to reading Maugham. A passage about Cronshaw —
the poet who drinks himself to jaundice
in the cracked booth of a bar . . .

I think of him now, tilting warm beer as the green grows
inaudible and petrels shed their silhouettes. My partner
sweeps the ute around a bend to aim us finally for this
island's crux — the nested midlands where our guide says
. . . *storms are rare but often savage*; where pioneers once
died in dozens chasing the thinnest hints of gold . . .

## Goats

*for Johanna Emeney*

Don't tether your goat
all alone to trim
your roadside.

Give her a friend
and talk to her or
she'll be depressed.

Put an open
hand to her brow
for a push-of-war.

Not good to goats
the Bible God
separates them from

favoured sheep that
they may be scapegoats
stoned for our sins.

I prefer to give
thought to Capricorn
who suckled

Zeus destined
to be chief god on
Mount Olympus.

Then there's Pan
half-goat half-man
who in Arcadia

plays his pipe to
fields and forest glens
and running streams

inspiring shepherds
with dreams of
beautiful women.

Picasso's sculpted
goat was once two
ceramic jugs,

one wicker basket,
scrap wire, palm fronds
and vine-wood horns —

but there's a shot
of a young goat
asleep on his lap.

Warned of the wolf
but craving free air
and the mountains

Daudet's brave goat
escaped and is
honoured in Provence

for her night-long
fight lost only as
the sun came up.

In this shot Jo
and her goat Rosie
are conversing

about Daudet
Darwin and the kinship
of species —

but there's a smiling
one, both saying 'Cheese'
(goat of course).

Jack Ross

# Zero is lying down today

but little specks of blood
on the bedspread
make me think

she may have run into
one of her twin nemeses
last night

*Yellow*
a big green-collared
glutton

or *Brindle*
a raccoon-tailed
bully

each of whom
sneaks in the back door
several times a day

to eat her food
she jumps out
hisses at them

but is only a little cat
once or twice we've seen
them ganging up on her

unable to help her
unless it's in plain sight
I suppose that's it

Zero
is now the thing
we most fear losing

yet cannot safeguard
threaten to crush
with the sheer weight

of our love

Cindy Botha

## Some days I want to un-bury my dead dog

out of that sleep. I don't of course, I let him lie
beneath the kōwhai tree
which scatters yellow grave-flowers
he doesn't see.

I want to gather up his gentle bones, my arms full
of skeleton whittled white
and solemn in its blanket shroud —

tibias like tokotoko, quiet coop of ribs,
his worn-down teeth snug
in my pocket's little cheek.

I hanker for the knob of head
warm on my knee, imagine his skull laid in my lap,
a hand's span of brow —
enough to fall in love again.

## We go down together

We have no names for our ancestors —
not for the one wading through a swarf of wheat,
the sun sticking to the drystone walls,
not for those ones idling in the alleyways,
or passing the windfall of a summer plum.
We have no words for the one with the machete,
sat fever-trembling in the Sumerian paradise
with carnelian pears and cattle shit and willpower
that looks back twice before walking into the lake.
We all have stones in our pockets.
There are no sounds where we lower ourselves
into the foisty mines of our grandparents.
There are no sounds where we blind ourselves
to the words text provokes, where we know
the paths of buzzards but can't break
the grapheme's hex. We have forgotten kith
and the torched hills, the witchery of gardens —
barrenwort and bloodroot that only a woman
could love. Our encyclopedias cannot speak
to the glisk of the campfire, the queer smell of kerosene
on the skin of one who burned a whole forest
to carry us. You and I take the stones
from our pockets, and throw them into the clough —
scrabble tiles spelling invalid words;
                                    animals;      exiles.

## navigation

quite a dance, that
coming down the creek on dusk
bootskate on electric stones
& gravity bullying us every step

I thought that you'd be over mate
in that felled tree way of yours
yet you knew the landlie like you'd cut it
laughing off the river's blind-bend taunts

you go through life that way
fate's map, creasebound in your back pocket
sneaking glimpses more to confirm
than to predict

Joanna Preston

## Clemency
*for my brother*

September: the month of your birth.
This morning the curtains mumbled at me —
fat and sleepy, a bumblebee the size
of my thumb's first joint
had dossed down for the night in their folds.
It stumbled across the peaks
of my fingers.
*Our parents are elderly*, you wrote.
*Whatever it was that I did, they need*
*you and me to get past this.*
Somewhere there's a photograph
you sent me long ago, of prayer flags, a glass-blue sky,
and the snowy scalp of Chomolungma.
Whenever I brush my hair, our mother's face
is behind the mirror.

In the garden this clement morning, the bees
are drunk in the rhododendrons,
rioting colour and scent, a hum dithering
at the fabric of the day, like the static
of background conversation
on a phone call from a busy café.
You sent me a photo of mountains
crowned with a shrine
and a military helicopter.
The refugee I found this morning
was large enough to be a queen —
a hood of fur around her face, dark
jewelled eyes reading the world
in a language I can't even see.
Did you know they've found
a bumblebee colony in the rocks

above Everest Base Camp?
Almost as high as you've been,
up where the air is so thin
snow and ice can't melt,
but evaporate.

When I opened the window
to let the bee fly free, she clung
for a moment, tapping her feet
as though sending a message in morse,
or the way a climber tests the ice
at the edge of an alpine crevasse.
*Whatever it was I did* . . . tell me,
what holds between us
other than blood?
We were born in a land so old
the mountains
had worn down to their bones.
The mountain you long for
is young and fierce,
and claims six climbers each year.

Outside my window, pollen is falling,
a gold dust across leaf and stem.
In your mountains, the window for climbing
is a handful of weeks at the end of spring.
The buzzing sound in your ears
is caused by altitude sickness.
I've written you up to the plateau,
Camp Four — the South Col.
It is midnight, and time to begin
the ascent.
Each spring a bumblebee queen

begins anew alone —
finds a nest for herself, raises the first
of her brood in a silent catacomb.
Climb. I will write your axe
biting, your gloved hands sure
on the ropes, the strain
on your arms and your lungs.
Soon the sun will rise
and trickle its honey across
the snow. Climb. There is
bad blood between us.
The buzzing you feel
is hypoxia; too little air.
You don't have much time.
Climb. I still don't know
if I will write you back to safety
or leave you there.

Robin Peace

## On being asked to speak as an 'emerging' 'queer' 'poet'

Mary gave my name to Mary —
so let's blame the Marys for a moment here

— you asked, I think, Jackson, just why
I was coming out after all these years?

There's nothing in the coming out of it, just
a poem I wrote about a father being queer.

Mary 1 liked the poem about the father
and when Mary 2 asked for the name

of new and emerging queer she gave
up the poem and with it my name —

odd we are stuck with the poems
we write, as if they were us. But then I thought,

well, I am that thing myself, bent in the middle
like a 50s stick scoffing the playground dirt

of a singsong chant because I would not wear
a dress and paid out the barber to cut my hair

— a short back and sides
with a cowlick for half a crown —

What was my mother thinking
to give in to that?

I was queer enough, too, in the 60s,
— though nobody used that name —

it was still too dirty a thing to be said out loud
and I didn't know to call myself that thing,

and the 'L' word sent titters of shock
when my back was turned, which I heard

and swallowed down like the shame
of pigtails, gym frocks and girdles.

I learned to slide sideways in stillness
and keep to myself well out range.

And the stillness became the in-between way of it
even when bars and booze and motorbikes

made speed and danger full of the thrill of it.
I'd already gone in, by then,

and closed the public door —
opening only in private and sometimes.

I've always been fully queer in myself. The plumber,
for example, knows that I'm queer, and the mailman,

— but I think they call us 'the girls', as if, in the country,
we are somehow more tame in diminishment and plural —

and for colleagues at work it's no secret,
just never the first 'who' of me that they meet.

And there's still the odd sneer and the 'sir' of it
and the gobs of hate spat on the street, but

it's been more of a personal than public story,
and it's odd to be here, today, at the front.

Mostly, Jackson, to answer your question,
I have simply been passing

as a cicada — waiting in the cool of the earth
for the moment when the sun is angled

just so and it's warm enough, like now,
to emerge to a queerer public life —

crawled out on a branch with my voice
and my stubs of small, blunt wings.

## Galilee[1]

For you I will stand
in front of the bulldozers

lay myself over
the entrance to the reef
wait for years in an outback jail

for you, for all of the children
and everything that is beautiful

the brilliant bloom of coral
the skyburst of the parrots
through the trees

for tomorrow
for today
forever

I will cut the fuse
pull the pin on the hand grenade

I will take the rubber bullets
the sting of the gas

and cry all the tears
that need to be shed

I will lie on the ground
on top of the coal seam

and stamp my feet
and punch my fists

---

1   The Galilee Basin in Central Queensland, Australia, where coal company Adani
    proposes a network of large coal mines.

and never never never let go

I will give my life for you
and the dugongs
the dolphins

the angelfish
their curious eyes
through the shimmering anemones

the trusting innocence
of all small things

all the snow
all the seasons

the ordered annual unfolding
of photosynthesis
and new birds' wings

your hand-reared calf
and your pet lamb

I will chain myself to trees
glue my wrists to the drill rig

cut the fences at night
under the razor wire

renounce my citizenship
become a stateless person
my heart all over the world

they will take the sky from you
over my dead body.

## Holy Relic

ubiquitous gusts    buffet solitary figures

one man chooses to ignore the hunting antics of a hawk
the changing photosynthesis of a leaf

another man    tracks    curative gum
seeping from the welts of trees

& another has seen the jawbone of a saint
halo-wrapped in glass

children    jump to the alertness
of a mountain    they run clean to the sea
past graffiti

scoured into cliffs    a mirage
shimmers in its hothouse of clouds    two boys

enclosed by this season's circuitry    shoot basketballs

through one golden hoop & then the other

Owen Bullock

## **sustainability quiz**

cypress leaves
brush cool
against skin

in the heat
ants traverse the mound

his sneeze through the tunnel . . .
jazz trumpet

the butterfly as though
it doesn't know the way

shade of trees
bigger than a family

summer walks . . .
looking forward to the scrunch of leaves

under trees
the scent of burial

at the lake
the water's nine millionth lap

snagged on native grasses
a sustainability quiz

the butterfly
colours a man's feet

a hopeful lunge
at the basketball hoop

apartments
fuck the skyline

## Road trip with my adolescent self

You say *what is the point?*
If a tree falls in Alice Springs, does it make a sound?
The cattle truck rattles past our '89 Holden.
Finches rise from the saltbushes. The day is a kiln-fire,
the soil — seven years sober and bone dry.
*Knock knock* you say, and I say *who's there*
like you didn't see the dingo and the death adder;
you don't see the glut of rust and zinc,
the bloodwood lifting dumbbells above the steeple
of the burnt-out gum, the sky dumb and blue
as the cookie monster. *What is the point?* —
like you don't see powerlines and powerlines,
hooves that storm the dead and the forgotten, lightning that licks
along the orange hillocks. You don't see what I see.
I need you to see what I see. You are fifteen
and the desert can only be a metaphor for absence.
Absence is a witchery, stark as a Baptist Church
hunching in the wilderness. Everything is hot and waiting
to ambush you from the sedges. *Knock knock.*
If a tree falls in Alice Springs, it weeps like a lost child —
who doesn't know where to turn when the starting-gun fires.
*Who's there?* Only the timeworn and the spent can hear them.

## mō ōtautahi
*for Christchurch*

me kāore tētahi ki te mate i roto i te ara taua
kāore tētahi

           no one needs to die in such a way
           no one.

I saw two swans regal glide
down the still lake
this afternoon.

they travel miraculous
one               well ahead            the other
b o t h       s e r e n e.

our dog a source of his own amusement
off on another parabola.

everyone should —
at least once —
inhale such harmony,
peace epitomised in epiphany.

me kāore tētahi ki te whakamatea i roto i te ara taua
me kāore tētahi ki te whakamatea
kāore tētahi

           no one needs to kill in such a way
           no one needs to kill
           no one

# No hay remedio

## No hay remedio

*'moving my life created by steel'* — *Frida Kahlo*

She moved her heart to the outside
She moved pins into her flesh and pushed

   *No hay remedio*

She cleaved her own ribs to make visible her rotten spine
She bled tendrils and was bound to the ground by vines

   *No hay remedio*

She lay on a scaffold between sun and moon
She scorched in the dead dunes

   *No hay remedio*

She was stretched on an apparatus
She was incarcerated in plaster

   *No hay remedio*

She was skewered and cut
She was buckled in and buckled up

   *No hay remedio*

Her foot went gangrene black
She suppurated from a hole in her back

   *No hay remedio*

Again and again she cradled her womb
Steeled and stolen the foot was gone

   *No hay remedio*

She wore suits and she wore frills
She ate sugar skulls

and she moved the brush — *VIVA LA VIDA*
and she moved the brush — *VIVA LA VIDA*
and she moved the brush — *VIVA LA VIDA*

---

*'No hay remedio'* ('there is nothing to be done') — a phrase often used by Frida Kahlo.

'. . . *moving my life created by steel* . . .' is from a comment in Frida Kahlo's diary relating to her painting *The Broken Column* (1944).

*VIVA LA VIDA* (Long live life): Frida Kahlo's last painting (1954).

Source for the above: Hayden Herrera, *Frida*. London: Bloomsbury, 2003.

## Waiting Room

the girl at the coffee stand
passes you a smile
fills the cups to brimming
with a surgeon's hand

no *how was your day*
in a place like this
just thin halls
and canned chemical air

just hours pressing on hospital floors
while people come and leave
like confused extras
lacking a script for grief

(the blue-coated woman
trembling with a nurse
*'she's been so long*
*without waking up'*)

cup empty again
plunge back into the elevator
where the cheery man stands
on the phone

his wife stuck dull with wires
in intensive care
*'yes my faith was tested yesterday*
*I could've kicked God to death'*

learn to breathe
one
two
that's right

you might grow used to this
you might get through

## Green Lane

Four am on Thursday, I drive you to the clinic
down Green Lane. There are no cars,
the barrier is up.

Dropped by the entrance, you give thumbs up:
third in the queue, you will be seen today.

I drove you yesterday, but a man appeared
from the car park, took your place
after I had left. I came back.

Five years you've had that wisdom
tooth rotting in your head,

keeping your mouth shut out of politeness.
They pulled it out in bits.
All you have to show for it, a black hole. Kid,

when you were under the sedative, did you think
you were in safe hands?

I cannot ask. The trees
on the return trip beseech the colourless sky
for answers. In winter, even the name is a lie.

## Superman

He runs when he can, Superman cape flying.
At other times you cradle his head
like the skull of a pomegranate
and think of cracks forming.
He's starfish-pale, pearl-smooth,
light moons from his hairless scalp.

This room's cards, balloons, the toy-animal posse
are an almost-home you didn't want. The nurses
know his favourite treats, the names of his dogs.
They know his pain, intimately.

You tuck your hair behind his ear
against his untraced brows. He's laughing
holding little race-cars up to your face,
fingers bleached as beach debris.
How easily you heft him, rock him
in a one-arm gentle creel. You're Superman too
though sometimes your smile fizzles. Then
you rip open your shirt hoping for a miracle.

His arm and stomach sprout tubes
while hospital fluorescents chalk shadows
in armpits, at ankle bones,
press pastel thumbprints on his eyelids
as he sleeps
but leaning in to kiss his cheek,
you discern the delicate tips of growing lashes.

## In the Rest Home

I
In between the living and the dead,
the liminal, the bardo,
I walk through the lounge at games time.
A semi-circle of chairs, Bing
Crosbie croons.
Beryl lolls, holding a ball.
Rabon says, throw it, Beryl.
Well done. One point to you!
Joan sleeps, mouth open. Her chin trembles,
tucks into her neck like a folded hanky.
Fred clutches the ball, a grenade
in his gnarled bombardier's hand.
His bandaged foot sticks out like a salute.
Throw it, Fred. He glares, hand tightening.
I'm glad someone's angry.

II
In the corner Peter hunches over the crossword.
He's a rangy, blue-jeaned fellow. Beside him
sits Mary. Still, regal, a waxwork doll with hooded eyes.
She's had Alzheimer's for ten years.
He keeps her company, feeds her.
The children can't stand visiting, so don't.
He says she's in there somewhere.
This is a place of forgetting.
Are you what you remember?
If so, Mary's already dead.

III

Dad and I trundle past.
He thinks games are stupid. Can't hear anyway.
Eyesight dodgy.
Look at these old people!
They've one foot in the grave, he said.

IV

My brother rode down in the lift
with a corpse on a gurney.
Hop in, said the ambulance man.
There's room for all of us.

## Evening Star

The Road to Te Whetu
      is made at night along an unlit path in black-heeled boots
*But do you really know where you're going?*           remember
              we've been here before         and it will be fine
               it will be fine.
At reception the nurses are kind       at the locked doors they are not.
        *We can't let you through because you just never know what you'll*
*see, and some people might find that disturbing*        *ok*
        but from where I'm standing it's hard to tell who is in and who
is out.
The Road to Te Whetu
      is made alone in the lull of a Saturday afternoon between  rain
showers in the same black-heeled boots
           this time they let him out.
We stand out front with a Somalian refugee, smoking
      my brother opens his pouch, I shake my head
             *I try not to do that anymore*      I try.
Before I leave I give him a tray of sushi        *I love you*
      *I love you*             touch his cheek
          see in his thick lashed eyes a shadow
        as if he remembers me from when we were children
              as if he sees who I am.
I walk away and he says not unkindly,
        *You're a weird little girl, why did you come?*

## The Dog Days are Over Now

We buried him deep
in the garden.
We buried him

in the heart of winter.
They closed his eyes
like the last pages of a book.
I couldn't look
too long,
but I know Mum planted
him near a dogwood
that we hoped would flower
in spring.

Oh how life brings you
everything if you wait.
Life brings you a dog
tearing the lawn to pieces of mud.
Life brings you a dog chewing
everything to ruin.
Life brings a dog with
a smile that he can't keep inside him.
Life brings the dog a family
and rabbits to chase into holes.
Life brings death
and a hole for the dog
and the rabbits now
make holes near where he lies
in a karmic twist.
The list goes on.

I don't believe in death anymore,
now that he's in the earth. I believe
in things
changing shape,
the rain becomes the mud, the mud becomes the grass,
the grass becomes the air
and the air becomes the rain.

I believe
his warm days
may have raised him a bit
on the karmic chain.
It is raining now as these words
rain from my brain onto this bored keyboard
with not much between.

The grass now green,
his bones not alone,
worms turning
in his grave.

The dog days are over now.
March marched in to April.
Time climbs into everything.
I sing his name,
I sing him bringing
me this poem,
I see him running like a mad thing
across the estuary
barking at the birds,
barking at the big deep sky with herds of clouds.
Though the dog days are over now.
The dog days are over now.

## Sumásala sa oras

The day before the money hits your account can be the hardest. Down to the last can, the last slice, the heel of bread so hard to chew, your inventiveness running out. I can't remember, were you at my flat or were we at yours? Two students at separate places, right before we moved in, our poor happinesses. Our destitute joys. We didn't starve, only flirted with it, hungry for something but willing to party, treating the microwave like a teevee station, watch our food spinning in a tease, a seduction, and you smiling and eager and laughing, and the food goes ping, and it comes out, your eyes bigger than plates

Sumásala sa oras: Filipino idiom meaning 'does not eat three meals a day because of poverty' (literally, 'missing the hours').

## Seeing silence for the first time

If silence came alive on the page
its corpse would sit up.

If silence came alive on the page
galaxies could not contain it.

If silence came alive on the page
poetry and physics would dance.

If silence came alive on the page
it would speak all languages.

If silence came alive on the page
nations would sue for peace.

If silence came alive on the page
the first would be last, the last first.

If silence came and lived on the page
I would hide in the hem of her folds.

Sue Wootton

## Anatomy

How closely seamed it is, a continuum.
Where does a blade begin? At the sternum.

Xiphoid notch, manubrium. Slit and peel.
Tease ligament from bone, lift silver sheets

of fascia to reveal the marbled meat.
Stranger and stranger this terrain: complete

exposure, full erasure, of the human frame.
Tracks carved into clay by rivers, rivers gone.

Where's the flow, the hiss, the whisper, roar?
Where are they kept, the stories in the core?

Where is the core? Turn out the heart. Shake the tongue.
Dismember hand and foot and wring the lung.

Where's beheld, believed, beloved? Where went war?
Where politics? Where petrichor? The slab is bare.

The scalpel hovers over air. Where is the ache
that galvanised this thing to move and speak and make?

Ivy Alvarez

## Sumugbá sa ningas

first our bones crack because they're growing and now because we're breaking, first slowly and then at speed, the crack and stretch to unkink the kinks, you rotate one way and then the other, there's a fire in the joints and an itch, a tiny scratch, put out by prescription, by painkillers otherwise known as alcohol, otherwise known as travel, otherwise known as distraction, or exercise, or sex, or forgetfulness, or changing your mind, or not knowing why in the first place, this distant friend always leaving you but bones are meant to ache, they cannot stay hidden forever

---

Sumugbá sa ningas: Filipino idiom meaning 'to rush headlong or impetuously into some danger' (literally, 'went straight to the flames').

## my own sad, ordinary, ugly human grief

it is not beautiful, it is workaday
it is not a soaring exemplar
of our very best

no artisans hewing through centuries
their sins forgiven
and their sons

no gargoyles chuckling and choking
so very like much this one or that
a sly joke for a waterspout

i am not awestruck
by an ineffable kaleidoscope
of coloured glass

this is as simple
as a drink of water
on a friday afternoon

the kind of carpet
underfoot
that can be galvanic

stroke it the wrong way
it will make your hair
stand up on end

our lady of paris is singed
a spire topples

i am unusually grim
during the livestream

I wanted what happened to be something

I could know

and I wanted what I knew to be something

I could describe

something to which others could say

I know this

this happened to me also.

At the back of the room is a mirror

dreaming it's become itself at last.

I keep walking

as if I know all the parts

and could play them.

I tell myself it's okay to just sit here

and breathe

over and over.

I taunt myself when I feel dirty with guilt.

I'm too busy stifling my anger to see what's causing it.

I want fixed terms by which to measure my experience.

I must be either high, or dying.

I don't want to know many small things.

I want to know one big fucking thing

and call it either shame, or home.

Leola Meynell

## Lena

Procurements from another's life
Paper — illness — illness — paper
I protest against caring
As though it is a crime

Purple autumn light
Snapped and torn, we fall
Beneath the weight of denying
Our goodbyes

# The Alchemist

The silver mining town of Guanajuato
is the birthplace of Diego Rivera.

His house is like an alchemist's grotto
metallurgy books line the family shelves.

His mortar, pestle, and painter's palette
mix all the colours of an afternoon dream.

His bedpan is the melancholy blue
of a river and red as a prickly pear.

Paintings on both sides of cardboard reveal
bohemians and Sisters of Charity.

Candy skulls of Diego and Frida
decorate his day of the dead offering.

Marigolds and mescal left in memory
of the alchemist turning life into gold.

# Other side up

Ruth Arnison

## Other Side Up

*for L. E.*

*This ticket is not valid unless placed*
*on dashboard with the expiry time visible*
*outside the vehicle, failure to do so may*
*render you liable for prosecution.*
*Please recycle this ticket as paper.*

Pay at any meter machine on a Dunedin street
and you'll receive a poem, gratis.

Today there were 2.5 poems on my $3 receipt.
*Carry On, Other Side Up*, and the incomplete,
*The Tomb of the Unknown Poet.*

When I returned, 55 minutes later, I discovered
that *Other Side Up* was not a poem,
but a set of instructions.

It appeared the parking warden didn't want to peruse
a poem to ameliorate her Monday morning malaise.

She wanted to see my expiry time (I have no idea
when that will be), and when that wasn't visible
she decided to render me liable, and carry on.

Promoting your *Carry On* cost me $40.00 my friend.
The ticket won't be recycled as paper, but kept
as a memento of sorts.

Robert Sullivan

## Conservation

The blue penguins have little wooden boxes
placed in mounds near the tourist stadiums.
I went to watch them coming home
from their ocean commute — waddling in single file,
pairs and clusters up to their enclosed area
where we'd watch them slide or fall down the mounds
squawking to each other. I was in the cheap seats
so it only cost me $35 for a single ticket.
I wish I was in the expensive seats
cause the penguins would waddle right by them.

Johanna Aitchison

## The girl with the coke can

in the cubicle
beside the window on the third floor of the
Massey University library yells out 'fuck!',
then 'sorry!', as a sparrow shoots across
the worn, beige carpet. 'You don't need
to say sorry; it happened to me last week,'
you say to the girl about the sparrow, which
came like a mouse, so close to the ground,
you thought it was running not flying. It was
the brownness plus the speed which startled
you, as if a mouse could suddenly sprout
wings, as if you might see, on the concourse,
mice fluttering up into the branches of the
golden elms, as if, instead of busy sparrows,
which turn their heads as if deep in thought,
you might look out the glass to see the
whiskers of a mouse, its soft brown fur,
wings grafted onto its compact body, tail
curling around a branch, as if to say
*back off, lady, this branch is mine!*

## Surviving the Ballistic Missile Warning, on the Windward Side

What's most astonishing about surviving the missile
        warning is not the sudden intake of breath
after learning from the radio the alert was an accident.

The rattle and cranking of opening jalousies and first
shouts of children released into a day proclaimed safe
                among brittle televised recriminations
and calls for punishment broadcast by politicians

and other talking heads is not a surprise. The silly
exhilaration of sunshine and the absolute attention
        required to the itch and grittiness of cat litter
beneath a bare sole on the chill of bathroom tile is no

                surprise. Nor is stepping outside to watch
the slender steel tubes of wind chimes bump each other
companionably in the breeze from the sea and realizing
that clanging and pinging was the music of desperation

        only fifteen minutes ago. The heat inside the car
when we throw in the towels and cooler for the slow drive
                to the shore is no big surprise. No,
what is most astonishing on this morning of all mornings,

        glancing over and over up at a gratefully empty sky
surrounded by a million sights seen a million times but now
                refreshed, crisp and brilliant, is one man,
furious, behind the wheel of his rumbling truck, idling

        in this sandy palm-shaded lot, honking his horn
in the extended blasts of the frustrated and powerless,
cursing a family packing their car too slowly for home.

## Go, boys and girls

A windbreak which grew
to threaten power lines.
In daylight, the now shaved boles
resemble pale, institutionalised legs
above which the remaining foliage
droops and dribbles.

On the edge of night, my headlights sweep
over a mass breakout from Bedlam.
They have pulled their nightdresses up,
have cleared the fence
and are off into
the dark of the Coatesville hills.

From the confines of my car
I urge them on
as if they ran for all of us.
As if they,
or any one of us,
could run.

Jordan Hamel

## Tammy the Briscoes lady plans my funeral

wearing weathered garlands
black lace gown        heavy eye shadow
            she's ready

a crowd of underpaid check out assistants
in desperate need        of collective action
bang reasonably priced pots and pans together
I evaporate        through        the ceiling fan

buy my coffin at Briscoes        Tammy
        use what you can        first
donate my kidneys to kitchen appliances
so everyone can see        the Nutribullet 600 Series
        really is        *The Original Nutrient Extractor*

put my lungs on a display mattress        Tammy
let couples rest their heads briefly        pretend
        this        is what their relationship needs
        when we all know        what it needs is
a rethinking of its normative monogamous foundation
and a non-shamey discussion        about
        consensual choking        and pegging

        take my teeth out first        Tammy
forge the enamel into a ceremonial dining set
to pair        with the carved tibia cutlery

peel back my skin
                mince it        into pulp
make biodegradable circulars        then stick me
in every letterbox marked        'No Circulars'

I'm a marketing genius        Tammy
let my dying act be your green tick certification
your        corporate carbon credit tax write-off

that's it                              Tammy
tell me I'm              less than the sum of my parts.
I've been a bad, bad     sack of biological possibilities

no one really gets to pick their own coffin
            except me                              obviously
because this        isn't a poem
it's a                        legally binding contract

all the best lawyers are dead
they've been hungrily waiting in hell
for a case just like this
                    if you buy my coffin

from somewhere that doesn't keep
batteries next to prostate cancer fundraising chocolate
or have a 10-day Christmas Extravaganza

                    I'll see you in court!

I'm ok with being scared        every day until it happens
it comes for us all             Tammy

        loitering ethereally in the bedding section
haunting Egyptian cotton sheet sets
        decent thread count        $19.99 (plus GST)
offer ends Sunday        Ts & Cs apply

# How to Talk to Death if You Meet Him at a Party

Listen attentively
Laugh occasionally
Show interest
Ask questions.

Be loquacious
Be gracious
Be inquisitive
Be cautious.

Pause for thought
Remain sober
Remember manners
Be exact.

Make jokes
Talk small
Be serious
Breathe deep.

Make eye contact
Relax fully
If he likes you
you'll just know.

Smile often
but not psycho
Let go
Be tolerant.

Dance if he wants
but not slow
Beware his sly hands
on your arse.

And if he asks
you home
tell him firmly
no.

You are seeing someone else.

Helen Lehndorf

## Did you get my message?

I wrote it on onion-skin paper
fed it into the neck of a bottle and put it in the Tasman Sea,

I sent a carrier pigeon.
I slipped it into a saddle-bag on a camel's back
and slapped its rump.
I hired a town crier.
I yarn-fucking-bombed it.

You might avoid me but
I assembled you
like the villagers building the Wickerman,
all hey! and bristle.

We started simple and I made us convoluted.
I didn't mean to. If I entered *New Zealand's Got Talent*
my freak skill would be epic mess-making.

Once we were sitting together in a car
and the earth literally quaked and
you thought it was me, laughing.

You carved me a wooden spoon,
& I stirred all the wrong things.

Oh the wreckage!
come on down
to my shanty town
honey

is the best home-remedy for a sting.

Did you get my message? An invitation to my art installation.
I wrote in autumn leaves on the corner of your street:

*You were the loop of the fruit*
*the glow in the gloaming*
*the sunny shimmer*
*on the wall*
*of my shady lane*

Jack Ross

## Are Kiwi women

too controlling?
a question I've been asked
a couple of times

I guess it depends
on what you're
looking for

men are quite useless
really
looking at piles of laundry

and ignoring them
but turning a
blind eye

when you're on top of
things means
less and less

you need to be on top of
we put up
masking tape

around the light switches
to prevent
the paint

from spreading everywhere
even so
it has a way

of going where it needs to go

## Body Image

At 42, I wore a pink bikini at the beach.
A male stranger asked me my age.
At 62, I took a lover.
We enjoyed our older droopy bodies —
eating, drinking wine, getting fatter.

At 82, I'm enclosed in a closet
Disabled/Elderly
while Chinese women walk naked,
luxuriating in and out of water,
unconcerned.

A body that once
boasted its bikini-scar smile —
now lapped with an apron of flesh,
penguin-feet still visible—
is a skeleton coat-hanger,
just to hang flesh on.

*C'est la vie*
I laugh later
into my cappuccino.

Aidan Coleman

## Late

1.

as you change
your honking mother outside

2.

*carpe diem*
said the tattoo in the queue ahead

3.

we could forget
how celebrity you were

4.

the poet stresses
the *Star Wars* reference will date

## En route to the city

We pause at the causeway to watch inlet spoonbills gracefully
gathering breakfast with their oversized salad servers.

When pannier bags brush our early morning legs we toss
a startled, *share the pathway plonker,* to the speeding lycra lout.

The wind weaves through the Harbour Mouth Molars
like fine dental floss, before returning with a salt spray rinse.

Behind Watercooled Sports, rabbits freeze, sniff the air, then bolt
into their burrow, a deep cavity beneath a shipping container.

Overhead seagulls screech like terrified-they-won't-be-heard
stockbrokers trying to buy or sell shares.

We gasp as a head-down-txting teenager saunters across
the rush-hour road. Her puppy stops to take a pavement dump.
It isn't a retriever, nor is she.

Coffee aromas exhale from the factory, flooding the city
with an early morning fix. We treat our taste buds at Vogel St,
gathering hot chocolates into take away hands.

At the lights, a pendulum-ponytailed German backpacker laughs
as she talks. I can't translate; laughter was verboten
in Year 13 German.

Somewhere in the City scaffolding drops, imitating a quarter hour,
but the Office Max clock reassures us it's only twenty to.

We shiver as we enter our office. The heater has just kicked in,
a kind of side-line kick, and it's obvious from this side of the room,
it hasn't reached its goal.

Robert Sullivan

## Steam

You need great literacy and numeracy
to have a career in Steam subjects. This town
has a lot of Victorian architecture —
old grain silos, railway sheds, public
buildings with Graeco-Roman columns —
so they've named it the steam punk capital.
I like the arching waterfront walkway
that takes you to the penguins,
and look forward to when I throw a kayak
into the bay with its small yachts
and power boats. I haven't counted.

## All leave is cancelled

All leave is cancelled because the Prince is
getting married and he needs your support.
All leave is cancelled because the water's
getting deep and someone has to save the
drowning. (The Age of the Fish is coming.
All leave is cancelled.) All leave is cancelled
because they will not stop until they have
what they want. Yes, them. All leave
is cancelled because we're one dental
emergency away from destitution and we
can't afford honey anymore. All leave is
cancelled until every one of you learns
what a god-damned apostrophe is for.
All leave is cancelled because we need
to find the Fiordland moose — before it's
too late. All leave is cancelled until someone
gets me a drink. All leave is cancelled and
we will honour the inevitable truth:
love is dead. There is no after the war,
there is nowhere left to go.
Do not tell me it's not what you think.
It is. All leave is cancelled.

Elizabeth Smither

## Ruby's seventh birthday

We will go to the Mongolian restaurant
where Ruby will eschew — does she know

such a word, has she encountered it
in her reading? — everything but dessert.

The restaurant will be full of wild-looking men
with whiskers and hairy arms and loud voices

and riotous women who laugh and saunter
languidly to the buffet where

a circle of cooks are chopping meat
into infinitely small pieces with cleavers

and at the dessert grill another cook is
making pancakes and sprinkling them with sugar.

Ruby will have seven pancakes, one after the other.
She has dieted all day for this. She will inform

the cook it is her birthday and she is seven.
He will look up six times and say, 'Here comes

The birthday pancake girl back again,' and
'Happy Birthday, Little Pancake Lady.'

Remember to
understand
love

## (Hills)

Wherever you farm you can see
the hills from your south-facing window,
crammed within parentheses on the horizon.

From your feathered sill you hear
magpies and their onomatopoeia,
your father's cavernous snores
and a sheep coughing under macrocarpas.

Breathe fresh mist on the glass
and follow the spine of the fish with your finger,
a punch-drunk slap-happy line
along quake-raised mountains.

Notice him watching from the tōtara post,
Kahu and his carcass breath.
A silent space between violent words.

Hold his blood-preened gaze,
wrap your heart in flax,
bury it with rocks for warmth.

Kneel at your stained-glass window
and remember to understand love,
first you must never have known it.

## Gate 2B

*for D. H. R.*

The windows streak watercolour and through them the lines in the carpark look like fishbones. Like if you x-rayed a kahawai. Sunk its ribs right into the tarmac. There's a half-drained bottle of Bombay between us, our both sets of fingerprints smeared round the throat. Queen Victoria looks out from the label as you push your hand inside my jacket. Spread your fingers costochondral. Get them in between the spaces the way God must've done when he plucked one from Adam. Only I'm an atheist and they don't have God or Adam in your religion. But how can I not believe when inertia slides you right close on the back seat. Your hair like twisted liquorice rope. It plays across my fingers as the Uber driver swings us down Stanley Street. The road is mirror-slick in the rain and the lights cartwheel orange and pink off the puddles. Beside the letterbox I hear the suck of wet earth. Newspapers gummed in the porthole like porridge (a simile I know you'll find abhorrent). You taste of tonic in the porchlight as I feel for my keys. I put a record on and we dance at the foot of the bed till the needle drifts through dead wax. Through the space between the last track and the spindle when the album holds its breath. We hold ours too. Then you say *tell me something* but I can't think what, so we swim through the sheets till the room turns the colour of pewter.

And in the morning
your hair floats
on water.

## ki te tūāraki

e mahara ana ahau te rohe o tai tokerau
e mahara ahau nga rākau matomato
e mahara ahau ngā manu rōreka
e mahara ahau te rangi kikorangi
me ngā tuaone ki te onepū kōura
e mahara ana ahau ki ēnei mea.

engari,
te nuinga o ngā mea katoa
e mahara ana ahau
te karera
te karera
te karera
o tau mata,

    ki te takoto koe ki a au
i runga i te moenga ruwha tā māua

i he ra wera rawa

     tūāraki.
  te
ki

## up north

I remember the northern district
I remember the verdurous trees
I remember the melodious birds
I remember the blue sky
and the beaches with golden sand.
I remember these things.

but
most of all
I remember
the light green
the light green
the light green
of your eyes,
  with you lying beside me
on   our   worn-out     bed

on a very hot day

          north.
up

## Zane

he didn't read
but he built me a bookcase
with his hands
hands I want to kiss the palms of
but not smooth the roughness from

and I thought
isn't that love?

I had been looking for signs
so big in the past
MONUMENTS and
speeches

but here it was
in wood and stain

love is the one who didn't read
but knew it fuelled me
so he took what he knew
to hold up my chapters
my pages

Dani Yourukova

## I don't know how to talk to you so
## I wrote this poem instead

I wanted to start by thanking you for that nice thing you said about
my work, appearance, affect or miscellaneous characteristic.
I enjoyed the experience so much
that I shrivelled like an apricot in the sun
all the moisture in my body suddenly
and violently redistributed
like the platonic ideal of a socialist uprising.
I should have guessed my body is a communist
bread is regularly the high point of my day
and everything I build is made of paper.
Remember that time you touched my arm? Because
I do.
It was around two and a half centuries ago
and I didn't know how to process
that kind of uncalculated affection
so I lied and told you
I needed to go to the bathroom.
Bathrooms were colder in the 1800s
but I think it was the right decision.
I'm not sincere enough for love poems
and you're so beautiful
it makes me want to take out a loan
or vaccinate someone else's children.
You called me back I think
but I couldn't answer because
I was too busy hurling my phone into the sea.
I've found that you have to be assertive with your touchscreens.
They can sense your hesitation
and if they catch you in a moment of vulnerability
they'll spend the rest of their two-year life cycle

sending you updates on all of your ex-girlfriend's successful career
moves and waking you with high pitched sobbing noises.
Everyone knows that fear is stored in the fingertips.
I'm sorry about that time when you asked me out for coffee.
I really like you
so I had to leave town
and construct a whole new identity
out of second hand poetry.
I was hoping that a keen interest in literature
would prevent me from having to develop
a commercially viable personality.
That's probably why I missed you the other day
when we made eye contact in the supermarket
and I looked away before you could say anything.
I'm in the process of applying for an internship
on a six month arctic expedition.
It should buy me enough time
To design a plausibly casual response
to your Facebook message.
Poems are widely acknowledged as an inefficient
means of communication.
But I didn't know how to talk to you,
so I wrote this poem instead.

Semira Davis

# Punkrock_lord & the maps to I_am_105mm

I have your handwriting at home.

There's a poem here — of your maps falling onto my thigh.
>They land like moths. Silent. Unexpected in the day. Three
sheets showing skeletons of streets and your writing giving their
names.
Every W is curved instead of sharp. There is a star and 'My crib' —
and the times and number of the bus I need to catch.

I look for where the maps were tucked — before falling. See your
email there
in the handwriting of a fifteen-year-old girl trying hard to not write
like her mother.
>Red pen, each letter a bubble. Added space in the K like a pocket
of air.

It won't matter anymore that I was searching — this journal for
found poems
>Your decade-old paper is material.

I will write a terrible poem.
I will try to describe your handwriting without mentioning the
elephant in my head.
>That your writing looks the same.
>That every scratch of the favoured pen shares an angle with his hand.
>That you're born in 1986.

The poem will be terrible because it's not meant to be a poem for you.
>It wants to be another one for him.

But those maps — your maps — why do they want this poem?
>I kept them because they were from you: sitting at your desk

in the morning, dressed for work, and stopped, checking online-
timetables, to copy the streets and names and —
    I stand in your kitchen waiting. Watch you bent over the pen.
    I follow them as far as the bus stop — then get scared and catch
    a cab.
    And through every house-move, every clear-out, these maps
    were always kept.
Evidence. You are spending your time on me.

But in the end they're how-to-leave-you maps.
So this poem isn't for you, it's for him.

## Magellanic Clouds

| | |
|---|---|
| Location: | Avondale at sunset |
| Players: | 2 |
| Talanoa: | Orbiting the Milky Way |
| Album: | The National, Trouble Will Find Me |
| Hors d'oeuvres: | Ready salted kettle chips |
| Obstacles: | Manifold |
| Allegretto: | A little joyful |
| Narration: | On dark nights you can see two irregular dwarf galaxies with your naked eye/ visible in the southern celestial hemisphere/ they reach their highest point in January/ a myriad of star clusters/ nebulae/ at opposite ends of the living room/ not kissing |

## Walâng taínga
*after Kate Durbin*

the university bar with its aura of myth *the woman*
dark and grim like a dog at night *from Sunday school*
carpet soaked with beer *tells me about the angel*
disco lights and a smoke machine *by my right shoulder*
music and drums and synthesisers *and the devil*
I can feel it inside my ribcage *by my left shoulder*
a boy asks to dance when I sway *I could never tell*
drawn to the maelstrom *the difference between them*
unrecognisable as innocence *when I pray by myself*
decades pressed between two chapters *I say to God*
the danger lay elsewhere *You are really running*
a sound with the volume turned low *out of time*

---

Walâng taínga: Filipino idiom meaning 'deaf' (literally, 'no ears').

## On Loving Two Men

Although it is not publicly
known, I love two men.

I love the way you both
fulfil me in different ways.

My mind rotates between
the two of you

when I brew coffee in the morning
& wander through my apartment

greeting the sun & bidding
the moon farewell.

Ok, love is a strong word
& it's true I haven't said it

to your faces & that you are both
married, which isn't a problem

for me, but others may judge.
They will say that love

should exist only between those
who perform the sacrament.

Let's just say: I value you both
in non-instrumental ways.

Let's just say: you help me
discover myself

& I am overcome with
fondness & affection

when my mind crosses
into thoughts of you.

Let's just say: I am
confounded by your plurality

& the multiplicity of yous
makes me multiple too.

Walt Whitman would have understood.
I hope my love doesn't anger you.

Since it is forbidden in this
bipartisan world to love two men

without boundaries or walls,
in the way that I love you —

since our bodies feign divisions
like Democrats & Republicans

filibustering on Capitol Hill, morbidly
repeating the axioms we learned in school —

I will mutter my refrain
beneath my breath.

My upper lip will whisper my affection.
My lower lip will make me mute.

## Signs

At the base of the brittle brown sapling
one that reads:

*For James and Haley*
*on their 5th Wedding Anniversary*

and the part of me
that doesn't believe

in the prescience of the world
can't help but hope

that somewhere James and Haley
are still going strong

have bought a cute little do-up
with space for the kids

will blame the brutally dry summer
the thrips and the borer

while the part of me that does
will watch the kāhu closely

as it ferries overhead
will lie sleepless

listening to the coded calls
of the ruru.

## Brightest first

in every tragedy      we place the brightest against
the one we regret to forget      and expect a revelation

to justify ink for the pages      a body for the cross
with the sureness of a straight line not known to end

perhaps this calls for an anthem      something akin
to a shield for the defenceless that reminds us why

we are drawn to      the richness of forbidden flesh
tell me      what marks the way      and when I next

recite the traitorous night      I will spend all the time
at my disposal      making it clear

I have come from a love so wild      there
are unmapped lands shifting      under my skin

places never seen      nor tasted      I dare not speak them
into being      by attack of claim or possession

I have tried to be good and just, but I have also developed
a habit to test the limits of what can and can't be forgiven

I have supped from a vein brimming with cursed warmth
a honeychain      a green door with my name on it

I'm in need of a border      an edge to push against
until it scrapes this filth from my skin      and leaves me

open to my own infidelities      the kind
that can't be measured or recorded      by the body

Elizabeth Smither

## Ruby at her father's 47th birthday

School uniform. Someone suggests she change
now she's home in readiness for the party.
Quicker than a catwalk model she's into

a white dress with huge pink roses
stiffened self-petticoat, white skirt lining
a pink sash worn high above her lowest rib.

She skips to the rotary clothesline, demands
a lift and someone to twirl it while she flips
over and hangs upside down, a socialite gymnast

and as the clothesline spins she sings 'Happy
Birthday' with a riff. On the lower terrace
her father raises his glass to her, salutes her.

Jeni Curtis

## you used to hold my hand

you used to hold my hand
the thrust of small fingers
petalled like daisies   white
around a golden centre   then
we parted   seas rose like barriers
between us   coral reefs
with bright striped fishes and
lurking sharp-nosed sharks   now
your hands shape into fists
against the world   fingers
tight   eyes closed to block
me out   a sullen stare
thus the teenage world turns

thus   the teenage world turns
me out   sullen stare
tight eyes closed   to block
against the world   fingers
your hands   shape into fists
lurking sharp-nosed sharks now
with bright striped fishes   and
between us   coral reefs
we parted   seas rose like barriers
around a golden centre   then
petalled like daisies white
the thrust of small fingers

you used to hold my hand

## Muslim Prayers

My udon noodles were longer,
thicker & probably tastier

than your beef tongue.
I never found out

because I forgot to eat,
as I often do when captivated

by someone.
I grasped the chopsticks

in my hand & watched you
check your watch

every five minutes.
You were working to a deadline.

There was something wrong
— yet also right — about being

together with you,
eating pan-Asian in St Pancras,

you telling me about your wife's
previous sex life & me

projecting my every thought
of you onto someone else —

so that our friendship would
never abandon its purpose —

& the Muslim formulas
that we repeated as infidels,

binding our heresies together.
*In sha' Allah.* If God wills,

there will be mercy on us.
I thought about how

it would have been to be
a sibling to you, or a lover

or just a friend, unburdened
by expectations.

I thought about your wife too
& the strength of her will

& you reading stories
to your daughter every night in bed.

All this passed through my head
as you stood to pay the bill.

A life lived well flashed before
me & I just wanted to tell you:

*Alhamdulillah.*
*As-Salamu Alaykum.*

May God be praised.
May peace be upon you.

Leola Meynell

## Comet's glow

Drawn in my mind:
the dusty lake your
grandfather led you round;
your slight fingers

plucking at dried hare's feet.
Also: the train of your breath
on the salt-bound breeze,
redolent with a coming storm.

Your words, fingernails,
belong to this place,
this leaking tower
with its bloodied bricks.

Look past me in a crowded room,
your glance cutting west.
Wild, uninvited, I still bloom,
lily in a patch of gorse.

C. K. Stead

## A Kevinish Poem for Kevin

*after reading* Keeping a Grip

A cup of rice and two of water
bring to the boil and simmer
while you slice the big red onions
to fry in oil with bacon, sliced small or diced.

When the rice is right mix all in the big pan
adding mussels and oysters
(the small ones in tins are fine)
and stir, with pepper of course.  And no, Kevin

bugger the Lemora — no need
to be slavish. It's time the sons of Sargeson
taught him about wines — we'll have
the chardonnay. Now taste, and Hey Presto!

aren't we back at Esmonde Road
talking books and writers, hearing our Puck
holding forth, holding out against
this word-poor witless *fuck of a world*?

## To You, in Late July

In the winter, when nothing grows,
our tree drips oranges like dew.
Is this not what resilience means?
Holding your hand in the van
I swear I felt some heart throbbing
louder than yours.
Some pink and ready thing
beneath the skin of this season
waiting to cry out.
I give you permission to seize this thing.
To make it yours,
to let it bathe you
in whatever you need to survive.
As August tears toward us
do not forget your mistakes;
only remember them with understanding.
Look above you,
to the birds in their constellations,
last night's storm left far behind.
There are storms enough in you already:
Use them.
Let the electricity sing from your veins
and split the sky in two.

Wes Lee

## Therapy
*for Marie*

You told me later you were afraid of me.
You didn't want to take me on as a patient.
Suicide beaming out of me like headlights.
I was so thin. I wouldn't take off my coat.
And when I did, I put it back on,
then took it off, and put it back on — off
and on this way, then rested my hand upon it,
beside me, like a small dog.
Now, we live in the same coastal town. I often
imagine bumping into you. I could find you
if I wanted to. You told me I could call you,
meet for coffee, you told me you had
only offered this to one other patient.
The trouble is,
that time was like heaven opening
with its ecstasy, like talking with God.
Meeting in the world we would become real.

# Competitions

Poetry
New Zealand
Poetry Prize

*Poetry
New Zealand
Yearbook*
Student Poetry
Competition

*First prize*
Lynn Davidson

## For my parents

You were meant to die at home
suddenly, one of you stepping in from a walk
to find the other on the floor inside.

Then one of you in the garden
splayed on the earth and
the other in the earth already so
it's like you fell to them.

That's not how you went.
Things were more difficult than that.

We still talk, or —
to use the language of crossing over —
communicate.
Newly chaste.
Awfully polite.
Shy ministers of the invisible continent.

To cover the quiet moments
I start to knit a hat, and
in deep times,
like a Victorian daughter,
I rest my knitting on my lap.

We have about a hundred stitches to let go
of Alzheimer's and stroke
and pick up the daily walks down the goat track
to the beach, you two
ahead of me,
towels slung around your shoulders,
your bare feet finding their own way down
the steep clay path.

*Second prize*
Janet Newman

## Drenching

When the cattle come home from the sale yards
in the blue truck that clatters up the drive
they walk as in a daze. Some snatch at grass
glancing through cracks in the concrete.

Drench them now while they amble
easily into the race. Tomorrow, stomachs full,
they will gallop away from you
because you are a stranger to them

though in months, as each day you
open gates to paddocks of fresh grass
and in winter lay hay
on the ground before them,

they come to you, warm breath
on your skin. See them paw the soft peat,
worry the old scents where you buried
the drowned steer two winters past.

Until you send them on their way
to be killed, they grant you the grace
of their company, draw you in with flared nostrils
that pause over the bones of their dead.

*Third prize*
Michael Hall

## Fencing

Some days
My father had Mount Tarawera
On his shoulder
Some days he had Edgecumbe

Some days
The paddocks dug holes
Into him
Finding only a water table

Some days
The river brought his soul
Volcanic ash, soil
Alluvium

Some days
He and the sun
Leant on the same shovel
Wiping each other's brow

Some days he tightened
The horizon
And started hammering
As I held the staple in place

*Highly Commended*
Paula Harris

## the first 146 minutes of knowing Rawiri

the first thing he says is
he loves my honesty, which is a good starting point
since my tinder profile reads:
if you're looking for your soulmate or friendship, there ain't nothing
for you here. if you're just playing a numbers game and don't care
about attraction, keep on moving. my ideal would be sex with
mutual affection.

my profile also says that I'm waiting for Idris Elba to fall at my feet
which is the truth

he corrects his typos and I discover it's surprisingly hot when
a man does this and I tell him so and he seems pleased to hear this
and each time I correct my typos he responds with "sexy"

he tells me he wants a lover who doesn't want to meet his kids
    until he's ready
a lover with passion and her own life

I tell him I'm not child-friendly, he seems okay with that,
we establish that we both prefer the lights on

I don't ask him:
how old are your kids what do you do for a living why do you have
main custody of your kids when was the last time you had sex is it
okay if I never want to meet your kids please tell me you're not a
morning person

he tells me:
I like to eat pussy I like kissing I like touch I like scent

this is very nearly too much and I squirm and struggle to keep my
    hands from myself

we each stare at the other's profile pic and we are both oddly
   angled in them
so I tilt my head to try seeing him more clearly
and I like his eyes and his nose and his mouth,
which I guess means I like his face,
and even though I don't like beards I think I can cope with his
and I wonder what he makes of my photo
my head and body slightly twisted away from the camera
because that's what I prefer

I don't tell him:
I've put on weight since that photo due to antidepressants I'm afraid
I might cry the next time someone makes me come because it's
been so incredibly long and I miss being touched I don't want you
to come to my place because my house is a reflection of the chaos
and damage inside my head I plan to commit suicide within the next
nine months you will probably end up in a poem at some point but
hardly anyone reads poetry so it's unlikely that anyone will read it
and recognise you as this particular Rawiri

I tell him I'm heading away for a few weeks
so if he's only interested in a must-fuck-now situation then it won't work
but he's okay with waiting

I tell him I have an ileostomy and he doesn't know what that means
but can read in the word that ileo means small intestine
and a man who sees some etymology in words is surprising and sexy
and I explain what it means
and he's okay with it

he tells me he wants to go down on me
I tell him that makes me wet because it's the truth
he wants to make me moan
he wants to watch me touch myself
he wants to watch as I make myself come
he wants to savour me

he wants me to feel safe and comfortable with him
I tell him so far he's proving to be very sexy
he hopes he makes the same impression in person
I try not to get my hopes up
but behind my back, so I won't see,
I cross my fingers

Poppy Hayward (Year 11)

# ABCDEFGHIJLMNOPQRSTUVWXYZ

VARK. An acronym.
A name, a label, for four different learners.

Visual learners. They are lucky.
A single glance, then bam! It's cemented in their minds forever.

Auditories. Be scared of conversing with them.
They'll remember it longer than you ever could.

R. Reading and writing. Loved by teachers worldwide.
Hand them notes and there you'll find a perfect student.

Lastly, Kinetic. The words: watched, heard, read—it all goes over
    their heads.
Give them something to do with their hands however, and they'll
    love you always.

School? Where does school fit into it?

School. A place dedicated to learning.
It excels in teaching VAR learners.

K? What about the K? No, no K. They always forget about the K.

ABCDEFGHIJLMNOPQRSTUVWXYZ

## **Boston Building Blocks**

red bricks hold my vinyl collection
its building blocks ink this city in stone,
white enamel statues of history told
in technicolour tea, in railings of fog

like clockwork
blue bikes build skylines, parked
benches map the nation with soles
of empty feet.

watch     as the water runs
   as freedom walks on footpaths

bare as the blue line
blurred behind the sea
cultures invert the conical flask

a traveller, not a tourist
on Beacon Street.

Annabelle Fenn (Year 12)

## October

October: I could die right here —
in the crisp of spring.
April may be the cruellest month
but yours is by far the most vulnerable.
October, your long-overdue apology
is caught, a tangled rope in my throat and yet
these things they must be said.
I should never have kissed that boy —
not in the smell of your warm rain.
Should not have slept with my
curtains open so I could
smile at the stars, thinking of him.
October, I'm sorry! Your air is
an aphrodisiac — the smell of lilacs
is but love's cruel semblance.
October, for these guilts I pledge
my very heartbeat to you;
October, I shall not go on any longer
lest we go tumbling into the
snare that is November,
and never make it back again,
October.

## She is

Lipstick stains on pale skin. Cold hands under hot running water. Frayed edges on a second-hand jumper. Smoke passed from lips to lips. Dark nights. Cool eyes. She is too-bitter coffee and too-sweet chai. Frost in the dawn light. Flickering street signs. Pale stage lights. She is the intrusive thought you can't get out of your mind. A bus that never arrives. Ash on the side. Broken glass on abandoned streets. Cool air blasted from the car AC. Windows left wide open. She is the cracked sidewalk. Chipped stones. Tar melting in the middle of the road. The blank space in between the stars. She is hair swept back in the wind. Tunnels that end in the dark. Horror movies in the early hours. Smudged eye liner. Running mascara. Bursts of noise. She is seeing an old friend at the wrong time. Someone far too important to tell your parents about. Flat stones skimmed over lakes. The sound of cracking ice. Warm liquid in an empty stomach. Dog-eared books. Stained jeans. Freshly ground coffee beans. She is stumbling over her own feet in the dark. Calls from unknown numbers. Rain hitting tin roofs. Skin stained with ink. Crumpled photographs. She is the sock that is lost in the wash. Scuffs on leather boots. Burnt out candles. Flickering lights. The radio cranked up far too high. Over-chewed gum. She is sitting on a swing set in an abandoned playground in the middle of the night. Dogs barking. Moths bumping into the light. Shallow laughter. Burnt fingers. Cracking chalk. Feedback through an amp. She is just another hour till closing time.

# Essays

## Six New Zealand doctor-poets

We encounter members of the medical profession at some of the most intense moments in our lives. We permit them an intimacy with our bodies, lives and emotions that we allow almost no one else. As Jerome Groopman, a prominent American doctor-writer, reminded us: 'Medicine engages life's existential mysteries: the miraculous moment of birth, the jarring exit at death, the struggle to find meaning in suffering.'[1] Doctors handle their encounters with us in these circumstances in very different ways. While some seek to distance themselves from their patients, stressing the supposed professional objectivity of their role, others see personal engagement and empathy as crucial components, alongside purely clinical skills, in their care of patients.

An extraordinary number of such doctors use some sort of creative writing as an outlet for the intense thoughts and emotions engendered by their contact with patients and, in the words of American doctor-writer Peter Pereira, the 'densely compact language, metaphorical content, and synthesis of disparate pieces of information — images, mood, tone, sensory details' characteristic of poetry are the form they particularly resort to.[2]

A handful of successful doctor-poets have emerged in New Zealand, and in this essay I examine the dual careers and published work of six of them, to see not only how medical practice feeds their poetry, but also the way several of them view their poetry as contributing vitally to their medical practice.

The best-known doctor-poet is undoubtedly Glenn Colquhoun (born 1964), a general practitioner, youth worker and author of *Playing God* (Steele Roberts Aotearoa, 2002) — the extraordinarily popular collection of poems about being a doctor — and many later works. For Glenn, poetry and medical practice have always been intimately interwoven, though the relationship between them was for quite a long time an uneasy one. He takes up the famous, though now distasteful, claim of one of the greatest doctor-writers, dramatist and author of short stories Anton Chekhov, that 'Medicine is my lawful wedded wife and literature my mistress.' Colquhoun's variation on that is: 'I joked that poetry was the first girl I ever loved, the one I always wanted but never felt confident enough to ask out, and that medicine was the girl I got pregnant behind the bike shed and thought I had to make an honest woman of.' In recent years, however, as he records in *Late Love*, he has come to fall in love with medicine, too, and 'On my best days there is no separation between them at all.'[3]

Rae Varcoe (born 1944) was a leukaemia and lymphoma physician at Auckland City Hospital for over 30 years and is now retired. She won acclaim as a poet for her collection *Tributary* (Victoria University Press, 2007). Poetry, she says, has become one of the 'buttresses' of her life in medicine.

Art Nahill (born 1960) is an Auckland City Hospital consultant physician and medical educator who has published two volumes of poetry, *The Long Commute Home* (2014) and *Murmurations* (2018). His writing and his career in medicine have always run parallel, yet few of his poems are set at the moment of the medical encounter. Nevertheless, the indirect connection between his poetry and his medical practice is very strong. As he expresses it: 'On a personal level, poetry has always been a way for me to work through the issues of grief, loss, and death which I encounter regularly on my ward rounds. Though they provide no answers, the poems seem to elevate the "questions" surrounding those issues to a state of universality and grace.'[5]

Skin cancer specialist and academic Sharad Paul (born 1966) works in Auckland and has written novels and popular science and medical textbooks, founded a literary café and set up a creative writing programme for children. While most of his writing is in prose form, he has also published a book of poems about melanoma, titled *De Natura Melanoma: Poems on the Nature of Melanoma*. Though many of the poems are clearly intended to educate the public about the dangers of melanoma and the importance of regular skin-checks, the collection as a whole demonstrates great compassion for those who will experience melanoma.

Renee Liang (born 1973) is a part-time paediatrician at the Waitematā District Health Board and a medical researcher. She is also a prodigiously busy poet, playwright, multidisciplinary artist, arts journalist and community arts activist. Medicine and the life of a doctor are themes she picks up only occasionally in her poetry, which is more often concerned with the lives of migrants and ethnic minorities.

Finally there is Angela Andrews (born 1977), who trained and worked as a doctor before embarking on a Master's in Creative Writing in 2005. Her first book, *Echolocation*, was published in 2007. She is not currently practising medicine, but many of her poems reflect on her experience as a doctor, as well as the reliance friends and family members place on her to interpret and advise on medical matters.

In a succinct and helpful essay entitled 'Seven Reasons Why Doctors Write', American doctor-writer Tony Miksanek reminds us that 'Physicians witness struggle — disease, death and suffering . . . They have a rich pipeline of poignant images, unforgettable language, colorful characters, and vexing irony in any single day.' And he declares that creative writing is 'an opportunity for physicians to make sense of what they do'.[6] It 'allows physicians an opportunity to memorialize patients and colleagues'. It may serve as therapy for the doctor-writer, especially when they know they have made mistakes or behaved badly. In their different ways, our doctor-poets all confirm Miksanek's observations, bearing witness to their patients' (and their own) struggles. Non-medical readers are naturally curious to enter the minds of those who care for their health.

Glenn Colquhoun declares in one of his many riveting talks and essays on the poetry–medicine nexus: 'There is a desperate beauty in the failing body. Being afforded the view [of it] is one of the great privileges of medicine.' He insists that the medical consultation is a key source of his inspiration: 'The consultation is its holy place, a source of communion and a science lab for the physics we have not yet described that occurs between people.'[7] All our poets, in their different ways, honour the patient and indicate that they recognise the privilege they are afforded and the centrality of the consultation in generating their poetry.

The affinity between medicine and poetry is illuminated by several of our poets in terms of the way in which the patients themselves may be seen as texts for the doctor to interpret. Sharad Paul's poem 'On diagnosis' expresses this most directly:

> My challenge is to read messages that appear
> on the skin of each patient as they consult me
> Which lesion should be dismissed or removed
> Things hiding in nearly two meters of skin
> I look at some of the samples I've cut out
> some end up scientific gifts for dermpathology guys,
> but most of them I can let pass.[8]

Many doctor-poets have observed that, while their patients may think of themselves as receiving care from the doctor, the thoughtful doctor is also a fortunate recipient. In his introduction to *Playing God*, Colquhoun expresses his gratitude: 'To everyone who has ever been a patient of mine thank you for the absolute privilege. Thank you for your trust and kindness. Thank you for your vulnerability and laughter and entertainment. Thank you for the poetry. You have no idea how many times you have healed me.'[9] Contemporary American doctor-poet Rafael Campo is even more explicit in crediting his patients for his work as poet: 'My patients are in some sense writing through me. Poems enact empathy.'[10]

Several doctor-poets insist that poetry is not merely a by-product of medical practice, but also itself nourishes their skills as a practitioner. Art Nahill explains:

> On a very practical level, I believe that poetry makes me a better doctor
> because it heightens and sharpens the skill of observation and helps
> me tune in to the presence and significance of what is unspoken in the

medical encounter, the silence behind the words, if you will. I also think poetry makes me a better diagnostician in that it teaches patience and helps me sit more comfortably with uncertainty. The process of writing poetry is very much like the process of making the diagnosis of some undifferentiated illness, requiring time and space for the poem, or the diagnosis, to develop.[11]

Among Tony Miksanek's observations about creative writing by doctors is that it often treats 'themes that focus on medical ethics and boundary issues'. However different their medical practices and, indeed, their writing techniques, our poets have in common their preoccupation with the challenges they face, in the first instance, treating vulnerable patients.

Working with patients experiencing dementia is a recurrent theme. Both Colquhoun and Varcoe write of the distress they experience when they have to apply the mental status examination. Art Nahill writes: 'One of the most difficult tasks I have as a hospital-based doctor is to assess an individual's capacity to make decisions for themselves when they are suffering from dementia.' His poem 'Commitment', about a woman he has to commit to supported care against her will, ends:

> Her mind is a boat
> listing badly —
>
> I consign her
> to the sea.[12]

Another heart-wrenching task for a doctor involves dealing with a frightened child patient. William Carlos Williams and British doctor-writer Gabriel Weston have written wonderful stories on that topic. In a poem entitled 'Teddy — for a child with leukaemia', Glenn Colquhoun shows the doctor trying to manage a child's anxiety:

. . . Teddy knew that the thermometer was not sharp.
Teddy was not scared of needles.
Teddy said the machine would make him better.
Teddy closed his eyes at night.
Teddy ate his vegetables.

Teddy's small girl lay in the corner of his bed.
She was not so sure.
Her eyes were made from round buttons.
The fluff on the top of her head was worn
as though it had been chewed.[13]

Several of our poets reflect on the other stresses they experience in their work, especially in hospital practice. Rae Varcoe asks how she can possibly offer adequate time and attention to a patient newly diagnosed with leukaemia to whom she needs to explain the benefits and risks of chemotherapy: 'How Can I Tell You This in 30 Mins?' stanza 6 reads:

the chances of cure are one in two
do you want to have treatment?
The rate of toxic death is one in ten
You have two days to decide.[14]

And in her poem 'Room 17', Angela Andrews remembers being torn between listening to the moving thoughts of an elderly patient whose life is slipping away and attending to the fresh patients who have been admitted:

There are new admissions
on the ward,
people with new symptoms,

you worry about them as he talks of his daughter
— She of the sweet voice

and lovely laughter —
and his son, somewhere along Arthur's Pass
driving through dusk.
You look at his skin, its lost

Colour, and his chest,
still rising and falling
in the regular way . . .

Renee Liang picks up the wife–lover pairing first suggested by Chekhov, on which, as we have seen, Glenn Colquhoun composed a variation, to explain that she eventually found her medicine-*husband*'s insistence on 'absolute devotion' intolerable and came to offer her creative lover at least half of her attention: 'When I found someone else to love / I couldn't tell you. / I don't know why. / You found out in the end anyway / you in your pinched mouth/ prim pouted way.'[15]

Rae Varcoe is troubled by the admiration she discovers she has for the potentially deadly organic phenomenon she studies and treats: 'I am startled by the blue beauty / of the cancer cell'.[16] In other poems, she walks close to the legal boundaries of her profession in offering this advice:

First, you should own a wise physician friend,
a young one, the kind who could find
a needle in a brainstorm.
If not, rent one.

If you wish, consult a minister or priest.
(For myself, I would avoid those with vestry interest.)
Perhaps pay a little visit to the chemist . . .

('When Considering Euthanasia')[17]

She also writes critically of hospital systems, whether profit-oriented private hospitals, in 'Mercy, Mater, Mercy', or inadequately resourced public hospitals in 'Welcome to Our Hospital':

> . . . hold on, miss
> we don't do obstetrics here
> the ministry has tendered out the babies
> to a birthing unit in Berhampore
>
> orthopaedics is off, love
> we're over budget till November
> and remember it's Saturday,
> early closing saves on pay
>
> sorry, sir
> all things psychiatric are to be
> managed in the community
> I would be best pleased
> If you'd ask the voices
> To direct you to a taxi
>
> Now please leave quietly
> through the exit marked emergency[18]

These six doctor-poets are only the tip of a mostly hidden iceberg of poetic talent in the medical profession. Many doctors write poetry for themselves, but do not seek publication. Other medical professionals write wonderfully sensitive poems around their experiences with patients. Lorraine Ritchie has recently edited a collection, *Listening with My Heart: Poems of Aotearoa New Zealand Nurses* (Steele Roberts Aotearoa, 2017). The website *Corpus: Conversations about Medicine and Life*, hosted by the University of Otago, which has been publishing articles, stories and poems since 2016, is co-edited by Sue Wootton, a former physiotherapist, who has also published five volumes of her own poetry, as well as fiction. Perhaps most exciting is the promise offered by the medical students who take medical humanities courses at the universities of Auckland and Otago, some of whom have produced remarkable poetic work. I co-teach a course with Elisabeth Kumar to third-year medical students at Auckland, who are encouraged to establish a writing habit they will maintain through the later, even more challenging, years of their training and into full medical practice. The most prominent example of a medical student-poet is Maria Yeonhee Ji, a former student of ours, who is just completing her degree at the University of Auckland, and who was awarded joint third prize in the immensely prestigious international Hippocrates Health Professional competition in 2018, for her poem 'Thirteen Ways of Looking at a Patient'. Of this poem, she writes: 'I wanted to capture some of the unique ways medical students see patients and explore some of the complicated feelings I have had about their care. They're feelings that I've never been able to articulate in the professional environment, perhaps because they are so very coloured by my own uncertainty and vulnerabilities.'[19]

Complexity of emotion, uncertainty and vulnerability are, nevertheless, some of the key features of the work of doctor-poets of every generation.

## More detail on each of the six doctor-poets

**Glenn Colquhoun** (born 1964) grew up in a Seventh-Day-Adventist family in South Auckland. After studying theology in Australia for two years, he went on to complete a BA in English and Education at the University of Auckland. He began his medical training at the University of Auckland in his late twenties, but took a year off from his studies to live in a small Māori community in Northland, which provided much of the material for his first book of poems, *The Art of Walking Upright* (1999). He returned to that community as a general practitioner, and wrote the collection of poems *Playing God* (Steele Roberts Aotearoa, 2002), which won numerous prizes and has attracted a wide readership, even among people who do not generally enjoy poetry. He later moved to Horowhenua, where he is a general practitioner and youth worker. He has published volumes of poetry, autobiography, essays, speeches and children's books. He is a much-loved performer of his poetry at festivals and in schools, and has won many awards, both national and international, and held a Fulbright Scholarship in 2010 to work with doctor-poet Rafael Campo at Harvard University. To get a sense of the range of his published work, of his performance style, and of his many current projects, see: https://www.glenncolquhoun.net/.

**Rae Varcoe** (born 1944) grew up and went to school in Dunedin. She tells of how her English teacher engendered in her a lifelong love of poetry. She trained in medicine at the University of Otago and became a specialist in blood diseases. Her own career as a poet took off when she completed a Master's in Creative Writing at Victoria University in Wellington in 1997. *Tributary* is a collection of poems in which she reflects, from strikingly different positions and employing several voices, on health, sickness and medicine. She has published many other poems in magazines and literary journals, including *Sport, takahē* and the online *Corpus: Conversations about Medicine and Life*. She has retired from medical practice and is living in Nelson.

**Art Nahill** was born in Boston in 1960. He studied first at Harvard, then worked for some years as a high-school science teacher. He obtained his medical degree from the University of Massachusetts Medical School, and practised and taught general medicine in the Boston area for 12 years, before moving to New Zealand with his Kiwi wife and two children in 2005. Aside from his two published volumes, his work has also appeared in many magazines on either side of the Pacific. With Nicolas Szecket, he co-hosts a series of more-or-less monthly podcasts, discussions, conversations, and interviews intended to inspire critical thinking in medicine (http://imreasoning.com, now in its forty-eighth episode).

**Sharad Paul** was born in England in 1966. His parents were both medically trained, and returned to their native India to work as doctor missionaries when he was five. He undertook his early medical training in Madras, and came to New Zealand in 1991. He completed three years of general surgery and two years of plastic surgical training, including work at Hutt and Middlemore hospitals as well as overseas. He is now an internationally renowned skin cancer specialist who has introduced innovative methods in skin surgery. He has taken up the challenge of making skin-checks affordable for all. In 2012, he received the New Zealand Medical Association's highest honour, the Chair's Award, and was a finalist for the New Zealander of the Year award. See his website: https://www.drsharadpaul.com/.

**Renee Liang** was born in New Zealand in 1973. Her parents made the decision to migrate to New Zealand from Hong Kong in their thirties. After posting the poem in which she recorded her reduced commitment to medical practice, she undertook two postgraduate arts degrees. She has collaborated on visual artworks, film, opera, music and musicals, produced and directed theatre works, worked as a dramaturge, taught creative writing and organised community-based arts initiatives such as *New Kiwi Women Write*, a writing workshop series for migrant women, and *The Kitchen*, a new programme nurturing stories in local kitchens. Renee has written, produced and toured seven plays.

Her poetry is to be found in her books *Chinglish* (Soapbox Press, 2007), *Cardiac Cycle* (with Cat Auburn, Monster Fish, 2008), and *Banana* (Monster Fish, 2008), in many anthologies, and in her blog: www.chinglish-renee.blogspot.com. In 2018 she was appointed a Member of the New Zealand Order of Merit for services to the arts and was the *Next* magazine Woman of the Year for Arts and Culture.

**Angela Andrews** was born in New Zealand in 1977, and initially trained and worked as a doctor before embarking on a Master's in Creative Writing at the International Institute of Modern Letters at Victoria University in 2005. In addition to her first book of poems, *Echolocation*, published by Victoria University Press in 2007, she has published poems in *Best New Zealand Poems*, *Sport* and *Landfall*, and in several anthologies. More recently, Angela has completed a PhD in Creative Writing focusing on 'the intersection of poetry and medicine within medical humanities: how the being, knowing and doing in poetry relates to medical practice'.

———

1 Jerome Groopman, 'Prescribed Reading', *New York Times*, 13 May 2007.

2 Quoted in Joel Weishaus, 'The Physician as Poet', *Philosophy, Ethics and Humanities in Medicine* 1 (2006): www.peh-med.biomedcentral.com

3 Glenn Colquhoun, *Late Love: Sometimes Doctors Need Saving as Much as Their Patients* (Wellington: Bridget Williams, 2017), 23, 26.

4 Quoted in Sue Wootton, 'Poetry=Medicine', *Corpus*, 21 November 2016.

5 Personal communication, 8 February 2019.

6 Tony Miksanek, 'Seven Reasons Why Doctors Write', *Minnesota Medicine*, July 2011, www.minnesotamedicine.com/PastIssues/July2011/SevenReasonsWhyDoctorsWrite. aspx.

7 Glenn Colquhoun, 'Some Thoughts from a Doctor-Poet,' *Genre: Forms of Discourse and Culture* 44, no. 3 (Fall, 2011): 326; 332–33.

8 Sharad Paul, *De Natura Melanoma* (West Union, WV: Middle Island Press, 2014), 34.

9 Glenn Colquhoun, *Playing God* (Wellington: Steele Roberts Aotearoa, 2002), 8.

10 Paul Holdengräber in conversation with MD and poet Rafael Campo, 'The Arts of Healing,', www.youtube.com/watch?v=-LksXrCQN5Y.

11 Personal communication, 8 February 2019.

12 Art Nahill, 'Commitment', *Murmurations* (Auckland: Two Hemispheres Poetry, 2017), 40.

13 Colquhoun, 'Teddy', *Playing God*, 17.

14 Rae Varcoe, 'How Can I Tell You This in 30 Mins?', *Tributary* (Wellington: Victoria University Press, 2007), 48.

15  Renee Liang, 'To My Husband', 27 August 2006, marking her last day of full-time work in medicine, www.blackmailpress.com/RL17.html.

16  Varcoe, 'The Cancer Cell Sums Up', *Tributary*, 47.

17  Varcoe, 'When Considering Euthanasia', *Tributary*, 55.

18  Varcoe, 'Welcome to Our Hospital', *Tributary*, 40–41.

19  Hippocrates Initiative for Poetry and Medicine, '2018 FPM Hippocrates Health Professional Prize: winning and commended entries', hippocrates-poetry.org/hippocrates-prizes-2010--/2018-hippocrates-prize-for/2018-hippocrates-health.html (accessed 25 October 2019).

## The hard and the holy: Poetry for
## times of trauma and crisis

Last summer, a 22-year-old British backpacker came to Aotearoa and
never left. The world watched as the search to find this vanished young
woman culminated in a body being found in the Waitākere Ranges, and
the growing realisation that our shores aren't all that safe for women.

In the months since the December of 2018, lede after lede imprinted
in our minds that we are not safe. Not when we travel. Not in our
homes. We are not even safe inside the walls of our country's aged-care
facilities. A vulnerability grew from these multiple acts of senseless
brutality and inadequate justice in the aftermath. It was a weight that
many women carried as the onslaught of disheartening headlines
created a widespread sense of crisis. I carried that vulnerability, too, that
fear, when I went to study women's health for two months in London.
In the afternoons, the commute home from the hospital was a daily race
against darkness. Winter coat wrapped tight, urgency charging my step,
always alert, always wary. I never felt relaxed until I was indoors or with
a group.

It was during this time I also came across Trinidadian poet Shivanee
Ramlochan's debut collection *Everyone Knows I Am a Haunting*. The
middle section of this astonishing collection is comprised of a series
of seven poems collectively called 'THE RED THREAD CYCLE'. These
are poems telling the story of a sexual assault survivor — poems that I
haven't been able to stop thinking about now for months and months.


There are important things to consider when it comes to the publication
of writing about sexual trauma. Is the publication of such work exploiting
those willing to share their experiences publicly? Displaying victims'
histories just to feed the internet's insatiable appetite for trauma that
is packaged in palatable, bite-sized confessional works to be read and
forgotten? Is there a clear distinction between the personal and collective

experience, so that the voices of less-privileged victims aren't subsumed by the story (or stories) of the more privileged? What is the value of publishing these works?

When it comes to poetry about sexual trauma, there is inherent value in the act of publication. Sexual abuse is often described as an experience of erasure. In 'The Life Ruiner' from the essay collection *Not That Bad* edited by Roxane Gay, Nora Salem wrote that: 'Perhaps the most horrifying thing about nonconsensual sex is that, in an instant, it erases you. Your own desires, your safety and well-being, your ownership of the body that may very well have been the only thing you ever felt sure you owned — all of it becomes irrelevant, even nonexistent.'[1]

In Ramlochan's 'THE RED THREAD CYCLE', much of the imagery around the narrator's experiences does revolve around damage, loss, consumption, erasure, death: '. . . you learned that some flowers bloom and *die* / at night', 'he *took something* he'll be punished for taking', 'no one comes to blot you up from this novitiate earth / where *you're buried now*', 'There lies an *ache* / in the place I was *ransacked*.'(emphasis added).[2]

The publication of poetry that does not shy away from pain and anger props up the belief that these feelings deserve to be heard. In 'The Life Ruiner', Salem emphasised her need for an audience:

Why tell this story at all? Why contribute to the compendium of stories about girls being used? Why ask all these questions that don't have answers?

It's hard to admit, but part of it has to do with the need for an audience. We don't exist without other people; therefore, our pain isn't real until somebody else looks at it and goes: 'Damn, that looks like it hurt.' When you're lost in the terror of your own memories, or when your actions occasionally prove their loathsome hold on you, the antidote to losing your mind is to have a handful of people around who know your wound and will verify its existence.[3]

The publication of victims' experiences also provides a sanctuary for these feelings, which are so often dismissed or ignored by our society, particularly when possessed by women. 'Our society has a place for actual abusers: jail. There are systems and processes in place to handle them and rehabilitate them,' writes Lyz Lenz in her essay 'All the Angry Women'. 'The faith I grew up with demands forgiveness for abusers, but angry women? They must be silent . . . My anger was still homeless.'[4]

And it is the manner with which Ramlochan wields ache and anger in these poems that I find so remarkable. Throughout 'THE RED THREAD CYCLE', Ramlochan uses these emotions as instruments of choice, to probe and pick apart the absurd trappings of rape culture.

To evict doubt from their internal universe. To perform, in the words of Ramlochan, 'anti-muzzling work' against forces like the 'patriarchy; heteronormativity; the hypocrisy of insular, male-ordered Hindu societies and subgroups'.[5]

This work is done with fantastical, lush imagery orbiting about a politically focused barycentre. Poems like 'I. On the Third Anniversary of the Rape' show how vulnerability and intimacy can be sharpened and used as tools. The entire poem consists of imperatives, instructions on how to describe abuse so that words cannot be used against the victim.

Don't say Tunapuna Police Station.
Say you found yourself in the cave of a minotaur . . .
. . . with a lap of red thread.
Don't say forced anal entry.
Say you learned that some flowers bloom and die
at night. Say you remember stamen, filament,
cross-pollination, say that hummingbirds are

vital to the process . . .

Don't say I took out the garbage alone and he grabbed me by the waist
and he was handsome.
Say Shakespeare. Recite Macbeth for the tropics.

Lady Macbeth was the Queen of Carnival
and she stabbed Banquo with a vagrant's shiv during J'ouvert.

This poem is simultaneously a portrait of oppression and a treatise on self-reclamation that concludes: 'Say / he took something he'll be punished for taking, / not something you're punished for holding / like red thread between your thighs.' It opens the series with resolve, with honesty, with daring. Audre Lorde, in her essay 'Poetry Is Not a Luxury', explained why poetry is a need rather than an indulgence for women:

> It is a vital necessity of our existence. It forms the quality of the light within which we predicate our hopes and dreams towards survival and change, first made into language, then into idea, then into more tangible action. Poetry is the way we help give name to the nameless so it can be thought. The farthest horizons of our hopes and fears are cobbled by our poems, carved from the rock experiences of our daily lives.[6]

Ramlochan's poems achieve everything that Lorde proclaimed that poetry could do. They facilitate the process of knowing, accepting, and investigating feelings so that the explorations 'become sanctuaries and spawning grounds for the most radical of ideas'.[7] In 'II. Nail It to the Barn Door Where It Happened.', the speaker instructs the reader to spit, to 'carry out the unspeakable thing', to 'nail it to the barn door / where it happened', 'Take aim' with a weapon, 'shatter', and 'blast'.[8] These are powerful verbs that translate emotions into acts of securing survival, that in the words of Lorde 'coins the language to express and charter this revolutionary demand, the implementation of that freedom'.[9]

The freedom comes intermittently, complexly, and never all at once. But slowly, in poems like 'III. You Wait for Five Years, and Then', we see the speaker leave behind temporally, though not totally emotionally, the trauma of the past:

> The first year sees you gallop.
> The second year finds you shattering crutches.

The third year loves the shine in your teeth while you choose
for the first time, in a cane field.
The fourth year flows in forty rivers and lesser tributaries,
from the banks of the Caroni River where the body will be cremated
according to Hindu rites.
The fifth year watches you forget your fisheye stones
on the breast of the lover you chose.

In his personal essay 'The Guardians', Alexander Chee writes that
when it comes to sexual abuse, 'You imagine that the worst thing is that
someone would know . . . The worst thing is not that someone would
know. The worst thing is that you might lay waste to your whole life by
hiding.'[10] 'THE RED THREAD CYCLE' does the opposite of hiding. In
the last poem of the series, 'VII: The Open Mic of Every Deya, Burning.',
the speaker takes to the page to read their poem in front of a crowd of
spectators and finds reasons for hard-earned triumph and rejoicing:

Each line break bursts me open
for applause, hands slapping like something hard and holy
is grating out gold hallelujahs
beneath the proscenium of his grave.

There is nothing more brutal than brutality laid bare, both for the one
exposing it and for those made unwilling witness. It is much easier to
turn away, to prevent reality's glare from scorching whichever part of
yourself is within reach. You drink coffee from speckled ceramic cups
to wrestle joy from the folds of the day. You bury your thoughts in the
company of others, on pages that whisper of lives well lived.

But retiring into the lush grounds of ignorance is a privilege few can
afford for long. Only there, totally removed from the experience of
others, can you build the perfect view. And this view comes at a price.
For one day, a friend will describe being raped without knowing to call
the experience by its real name. They will do it matter-of-factly and

come to the quiet conclusion that it is in their best interests not to file a report. A patient will busy themselves in your clinic with the act of holding more than any person should: memories of what happened the night before; the fraying parts of their battered self; their dignity and resolve as they are asked to unclothe and be examined again, and again, and again. And each time it becomes more difficult to go back to that place with the view where all men are like those who have shown you love.

How then to tackle the fire without risking burning? In this regard I am not brave. Some months ago, I came across a copy of the essay I wrote for the medical school application. At nineteen, I dreamed of being a doctor who radiated kindness so wild that a retired coal miner would take one look at me and recall 40 shades of green. Now, in the final year of medical school, I know that this will be a difficult — though perhaps not impossible — dream. Physician suicide and burnout plague our ranks; you cannot endlessly tend to suffering without suffering in turn. These days, I am more careful about setting fire breaks between my empathy and open flame.

I believe that poetry has a crucial role in spaces like these. Like all works of art, poetry exists in a third space, a space where confrontation waits for you when you are ready. It opens the door to deeper engagement, but this door can be opened at any time and shut again should your mind require. And when you do choose to face the different kind of life lived, the indescribable experiences that lie described and somehow contained in their inky rows, your worldview shifts.

Nobody describes the way words can change your emotional and receptive pathways better than Annie Dillard in *The Writing Life*:

> The line of words fingers your own heart. It invades arteries, and enters the heart on a flood of breath; it presses the moving rims of thick valves; it palpates the dark muscle strong as horses, feeling for something, it knows not what. A queer picture beds in the muscle like a worm encysted — some film of feeling, some song forgotten, a scene in a dark bedroom, a corner of the woodlot, a terrible dining room, that exalting sidewalk;

these fragments are heavy with meaning. The line of words peels them back, dissects them out. Will the bared tissue burn? Do you want to expose these scenes to the light? You may locate them and leave them, or poke the spot hard till the sore bleeds on your finger, and write with that blood. If the sore spot is not fatal, if it does not grow and block something, you can use its power for many years, until the heart resorbs it.[11]

Poetry as energy, vector, explorer, unveiling . . . Poetry operates on the personal level, on the reader's consciousness, but its effects ripple out farther. If capable of changing the mind of even one person, poetry can be seen as a form of societal reconstruction. It is, as Audre Lorde wrote in the essay 'Poetry Is Not a Luxury', 'not only a dream and a vision; it is the skeleton architecture of our lives. It lays the foundations for a future of change, a bridge across our fears of what has never been before.'[12]

It is this fundamental structural change that poetry can facilitate which makes reading and supporting poetry like that of Ramlochan so important and valuable. In an essay deconstructing contemporary issues in art writing, Vanessa Crofskey wrote about how 'words can work as a structural form of oppression. The way we frame the world informs the way we interact with the world. It affects how we categorise objects and identities, where we put them on a value scale.'[13]

But words can also act as a structural form of liberation. Poetry that renders the dreams of sexual abuse survivors both dreamable and realisable, poetry that, in the words of Lorde, moves 'our spirits most deeply and directly towards and through promise' to a better, other side and contain 'the future of our worlds'[14] . . . These poems possess the power to alter our social environment. If we let them. If we open them up and hold on to and for dear life.

---

1   Nora Salem, 'The Life Ruiner', in *Not That Bad: Dispatches from Rape Culture*, ed. Roxane Gay (London: Atlantic Books, 2018), 151.

2   Shivanee Ramlochan, *Everyone Knows I Am a Haunting* (Leeds: Peepal Tree Press, 2017). 35–36; 41; 45.

3   Salem, 'The Life Ruiner', 152–153.

4   Lyz Lenz, 'All the Angry Women', in *Not That Bad*, 158–159.

5   Rajiv Mohabir, 'Coolitude Poetics Interview with Shivanee Ramlochan' *Jacket2*, 22 November 2017, jacket2.org/commentary/coolitude-poetics-interview-shivanee-ramlochan.

6   Audre Lorde, 'Poetry Is Not a Luxury', in *Your Silence Will Not Protect You* (London: Silver Press, 2017), 8.

7   Ibid., 9.

8   Ramlochan, *Everyone Knows I Am a Haunting*, 37–38.

9   Lorde, 'Poetry Is Not a Luxury', 10.

10  Alexander Chee, 'The Guardians', in *How to Write an Autobiographical Novel: Essays by Alexander Chee* (Boston, MA: Mariner Books, 2018), 232.

11  Annie Dillard, *The Writing Life* (New York: HarperCollins, 2013), 20.

12  Lorde, 'Poetry Is Not a Luxury', 9.

13  Vanessa Crofskey, 'There's Something Wrong With Art Writing', *The Pantograph Punch*, 12 June 2019, www.pantograph-punch.com/post/jargon-art-writing.

14  Lorde, 'Poetry Is Not a Luxury', 11.

## Works cited

Alexander Chee, 'The Guardians,' *How To Write an Autobiographical Novel: Essays by Alexander Chee.* (Boston, MA: Mariner Books, 2018), 232.

Vanessa Crofskey, 'There's Something Wrong With Art Writing'. *The Pantograph Punch*, 12 June 2019, accessed 15 August 2019, www.pantograph-punch.com/post/jargon-art-writing.

Annie Dillard, *The Writing Life* (New York: HarperCollins, 2013).

Lyz Lenz, 'All the Angry Women', in *Not That Bad: Dispatches from Rape Culture*, ed. Roxane Gay (London: Atlantic Books, 2018), 158–59.

Audre Lorde, 'Poetry Is Not a Luxury', in *Your Silence Will Not Protect You* (London: Silver Press, 2017), 8–11.

Rajiv Mohabir, 'Coolitude Poetics Interview with Shivanee Ramlochan', *Jacket2*, 22 November 2017, jacket2.org/commentary/coolitude-poetics-interview-shivanee-ramlochan.

Shivanee Ramlochan, 'THE RED THREAD CYCLE', in *Everyone Knows I Am a Haunting* (Leeds: Peepal Tree Press, 2017), 33–45.

Nora Salem, 'The Life Ruiner', in *Not That Bad: Dispatches from Rape Culture*, ed. Roxane Gay (London: Atlantic Books, 2018), 151–53.

# Jealous of youth

Sarah Laing

National Poetry Day 2019, I was waiting for a Tinder date to text...

GODDAMMIT, I'M NOT GOING TO WAIT BY THE PHONE LIKE I DID AS A TEENAGER

PLAN B: SEXY POETS!

Poets weren't so hot in the nineties

I should know—I was one of them.

THE PINK BLOOD SHOCKS

The audience was other poets

Readings were a fringe interest

I WROTE THIS POEM WHILST LIVING WITH JIM IN JERUSALEM IN 1970... IT GOES LIKE THIS

Mostly the poetry was terrible, and open mike

I LOVE YOU LIKE I LOVE A FRESH SCALPEL BLADE ON MY INNER THIGH

Although if you had a car, you could go watch the stars read at a Wairarapa vineyard

BILL MANHIRE!

JENNY BORNHOLDT!

GREG O'BRIEN

If there was a particularly good poem, everyone would sigh a little

OH!

JUST LIKE A MOUSE ORGASM, ASHLEIGH YOUNG ONCE OBSERVED

If you wanted to collect your answer phone messages, there was a special number you could dial

I WONDER IF IT WILL BE LIKE ANY OF THE POETRY SHOWS WE PUT ON

I HOPE THERE'LL BE SOMEONE I KNOW THERE

DAMN YOU, TINDER DATE, TEXT ALREADY

MONARCH TATTOOS

IS THIS THE HERA LINDSAY BIRD EFFECT?

NO, I THINK FREYA DALY SADGROVE IS HER OWN PHENOMENON

BADA BOOM-BOOM

... and then the show is over.

SHOULD I SIGN UP FOR POST POETRY KARAOKE?

DAMN, THAT'S THE KIND OF THING I'D'VE THOUGHT OF

The next day the reckons flooded in

Ben Fagan
For this reason, if I may be so bold, I reckon "show ponies: a @NZ poetry day extravaganza" was a watershed moment for poetry in performa in Wellington. As @FreyaD effervescent risks!

GODAMMIT, WE PUT ON CRAZY SHOWS TOO! WE WERE EFFERVESCENT! IF ONLY TWITTER COULD'VE SEEN US...

I compulsively checked my Tinder app in case I'd missed anything

SHIT! I GAVE HIM THE WRONG NUMBER! NO WONDER HE DIDN'T TEXT

I'M KIND OF GLAD I DID

## Boundaries are where connections happen:
## Some thoughts about essaying poetry

It is obvious really, but it took a little while for me to make all the connections for myself. It wasn't just one thing, but several things going on over time, and at the same time. This is not uncommon.

I had noticed that a lot of poets said they were 'writing essays at the moment'. And I had for some time been writing poems that I had felt were doing the same work as essays. And the poems I was reading that were getting me the most excited were ones that were definitely essayistic in their nature (especially Anne Carson's *The Albertine Workout*, which I return to later). Around this time the issue of *Landfall* with the winners of the essay competition came out, and most of them were written by poets.

Clearly there was some kind of affinity between poetry and the essay. What was it? And what's going on when they join forces? Something interesting. Something exciting.

I am interested in what one form can learn from another form, or add to another form. I get excited by experiment, by fusion, by riding roughshod over the rules. I am really interested, as both a reader and a writer, in the place where boundaries are, which is also where the connections are, and what goes on there. It was while reading about the philosopher Simone Weil that I came across the term 'metaxu', meaning a kind of point of connection and mediation: 'Two prisoners whose cells adjoin communicate with each other by knocking on the wall. The wall is the thing which separates them but it is also their means of communication. It is the same with us and God. Every separation is a link.'[1] She meant it in a more spiritual way, but I like the applicability of this idea to many things, including where literary genres meet.

Think about what isn't in poetry yet that you could put here.
— Patricia Lockwood[2]

I find that as soon as I start thinking about poetry *and* — poetry and the essay in this case, but poetry and biography (another interest of mine) or poetry and history — it immediately sends me to thinking about what poetry is. How to define poetry. This is something I think about quite a lot anyway.

Some people are quite certain about what poetry is and where its boundaries lie. I am not one of those people. I like not being one of those people. I enjoy seeing it leak out of boxes, being hard to contain. I'm interested in those seepages.

Every time I've tried to define what a poem is, I've immediately come up with exceptions — poems that don't fit the criteria, or other literary works that do. A poem has line breaks; except of course when it doesn't (we don't have to be especially radical to accept prose poems as poetry). We've long gone past thinking that poems have to rhyme, which itself was never universal anyway. Not every poem will have a strict form, or metre, or alliteration, or assonance, or metaphor or simile.

In the face of this, I have been developing a theory that poetry is simply what we *say* is poetry and therefore *read* as poetry — with more care and attention, looking for the features we expect in a poem, therefore finding them; much in the way that an object placed in an art gallery (arguably) becomes art, and is looked at and paid attention to as an artwork — as Duchamp championed with his readymades.

I do recognise that this is a slightly circular argument: because we have to have some ideas of what poetry *is* to know what we're looking for, but those ideas have come from poems we've read earlier. So, there are some things we can say usefully, if not universally, about poetry and its nature, and therefore what it will bring to this intersection with the essay.

We are on fairly safe ground to say that a poem is a literary work, made up of language. And in poetry we do expect especially intense or rich language, language that is aware of itself, that is more highly patterned, perhaps more rhythmic than ordinary language. Not necessarily more beautiful, though when something other than a poem is described as poetic, it does usually mean it is beautiful or graceful. I think we can also say that in a poem we expect metaphor and symbol.

We expect layers of meaning. We expect a poem to be about more than it seems to be about on the surface. When reading poetry, we expect to have to do some work, to make leaps, to be on our toes, to make connections, find subtext. We can cope with gaps, with fragmentation. Human brains are the ultimate pattern-makers, looking for connections and meaning in even disparate and random things. (A term for this, apophenia, originally referred to the way delusional people see connections where there are none, such as in lottery numbers.)

> [T]he fragment stands alone but speaks, or must be made to speak by a reader, to the fragments that surround it.
> — Brian Dillon[3]

And what of the essay? It is also a literary work (leaving aside such things as the photo essay). It is non-fiction, meaning it is about something real. The Oxford Online simply says it is: 'A short piece of writing on a particular subject.'[4] Brian Dillon more poetically refers to the root of the meaning of the word when he says: 'Imagine a type of writing so hard to define its very name should be something like: an effort, an attempt, a trial. Surmise or hazard, followed very likely by failure.'[5]

Unlike poetry, which has been around for thousands of years, the essay is a relatively recent interloper. Michel Montaigne, generally named as the father of the essay, only started writing them in the 1570s, though there are earlier examples of what we could call essays. Montaigne's style of essay tended to take a subject, muse on it from one side and then another, find relevant quotations from others who have thought about this subject (usually classical sources), wander off down tangents, maybe come back, and resolve that perhaps nothing can be resolved.

There are many different kinds of essays, of course, from academic-style critical essays which aim to convince you of their argument, to more meandering personal essays. At the moment I think we are in the heyday of a kind of literary essay that owes much to Montaigne, but which are generally less rambling. These are medium-length musings, often with an autobiographical element, that aren't necessarily trying to convince you of anything — where you feel you are watching the writer thinking something through as they write, and reading it re-creates that thinking in the reader. They're mostly beautifully written. They have subtext, they are often understated. Like a metaphor, they often take one thing and place it next to another thing, leaving us to find the connection, the resonance between them. It's beginning to sound a lot like poetry.

> That's what I'm looking for, that transfer, a new attunement. In the experience neither poem nor reader has yielded; on the contrary, we generate something together. It's because 'a poem is a thinking thing,' as my onetime colleague Karen Volkman said somewhere. It's a choice formulation: 'a thinking thing,' a phrase in which I hear both the poem's instrumentality for thought (it's something with which to think), and its processing of its materials (it's something that conducts thought, as if independently).
> — Brian Blanchfield[6]

But what I've become especially interested in are poems that *are* essays, as opposed to prose essays that are written more lyrically. Where the poem becomes a 'a thinking thing' — a site of thinking, a record of thinking, an enaction of thinking, a recreation of thinking, and causes the thinking to occur also in the mind of the reader. Where ideas are turned over, this way and that, looked at from different angles, followed down paths and digressions. Where leaps are taken, connections are made, arguments articulated, and possibly knowledge is even captured.

For a poem to do these things is not new — poetry has been doing everything forever — and the verse essay actually has a long and distinguished history. We can go back at least as far as ancient Greek poet Hesiod, who recorded knowledge in his works; most pre-Socratic philosophers, such as Empedocles, wrote in verse. Lucretius' didactic poem about Epicureanism, *On the Nature of Things*, could be argued to be an essay, as can Horace's *Ars Poetica*. In the early eighteenth century

Pope and others wrote self-conscious essays in verse, including Pope's *An Essay on Criticism*. The tradition was continued by the Romantics, and so on.

Not that I was aware of this history when I started thinking about the intersection of poetry and the essay. But the more I started exploring this idea, as a reader and as a writer, the more I have discovered that many others have been there before me.

I first became consciously aware of the essayistic in my own work when writing the poems that made up my collection *Cinema* (2014), though with hindsight I can see it in earlier work. At university, mumble years ago, I studied English literature and art history, which mainly involved reading or looking at things, and then writing interpretations of them, with or without (usually with) secondary sources. I started to see that some of the poems I was writing about films and film-making were sort of mini-interpretive essays about films, exercising those muscles that hadn't been much used since my university days. Except the poems were much shorter than the essays, and I didn't have to hand them in for marking. I also didn't need to make a coherent argument or fill in all the gaps. A much better situation, as far as I was concerned.

> The lyric essay partakes of the poem in its density and shapeliness, its distillation of ideas and musicality of language. It partakes of the essay in its weight, in its overt desire to engage with facts, melding its allegiance to the actual with its passion for imaginative form.
> — Deborah Tall and John D'Agata[7]

But it was while working on my most recent collection, *How to Live* (2019), that I more deliberately explored this place where the poem and the essay meet, as well as thinking about where other divergent things meet — where poetry meets prose, where fiction meets non-fiction, where biography meets autobiography, where plain-speaking meets lyricism, where form pushes against digression.

Among the longer essay poems in *How to Live* are: a long deconstructed biographical essay prose poem about George Eliot

('George Eliot: A Life'); an essay combining memoir about my husband's cancer treatment with an exploration of the nature of poetry and metaphor, among other things ('How to Live'); and biographical essays about female philosophers from the past, which also look at the places of women in the past and present, and how they have refused to be silenced ('Notes on the Unsilent Woman' and 'Ban Zhao'). As well as the individual essay poems, though, I also conceived the book as a whole as a hybrid essay that considers and explores those big philosophical and practical questions: of how one could or should live a good life, how to be happy, how to not die, how to live — to really embrace life — how to live through crises, illness and adversity, and how other people have lived. These were all things I was thinking through in my real life, and probably always will be, and, because I'm a poet, poetry is how, and where, I think.

And in poetry I can think in gaps and leaps and fragments, in accretions, layers, and from lots of different angles. I love the way the human mind, especially when reading poetry, can leap over gaps, make patterns and meaning out of fragments. And I can ask a lot of questions without needing to come to any definitive conclusions. Answers have their place, but my suspicion of definitiveness works well, I think, in an essay poem.

Excited about my new realisation of the compatibility of poem and essay, I of course started noticing essay poems, or the essaying impulse in poems, everywhere.

I was familiar of course with Anne Carson's celebrated long poem 'The Glass Essay', though I hadn't really thought very deeply about it as an essay, despite it announcing itself as an essay right up front. The technique of taking two or more subjects in parallel is a common one in both essay and poetry. The effect is to make the reader consider what the connection is between the subjects, to find links, metaphors, new understandings. In 'The Glass Essay', Carson uses this technique to weave a narrative poem about a woman (the narrator may or may not be the poet herself) going to visit her mother in the aftermath of a relationship break-up with meditations about the life and work of

Emily Brontë. We are left to make our own connections, and are also left with a better knowledge and understanding of Emily Brontë from a thoughtful scholar.

Another even more essayistic Anne Carson prose poem is *The Albertine Workout*, which continues the idea of poem as literary criticism but amps it up several notches from 'The Glass Essay'. The story of the narrator is pushed into the background, while the main focus is an examination of Marcel Proust's multi-volume novel *À la Recherche du Temps Perdu* (*In Search of Lost Time*), specifically through an exploration of the character of Albertine, with many asides about the life of Proust himself.

The poem is arranged in 59 short, numbered paragraphs that range around in topic, followed by 16 appendices (numbered from 4 to 59, so there are gaps where many were removed, or were unwritten — these ghost appendices offer unknown possibilities), which illuminate or add to some aspect of the main poem/essay, or possibly just spin off in their own directions. What has made me so excited about this poem is the way it sails right on past the boundaries of what we usually think of as poetry, and makes me think 'This is what a poem can do!' I often feel this way after reading Anne Carson, and there are many other examples in her oeuvre that we could think of as essay poems.

In several of the longer sequences in her collection *The Grief Almanac: A Sequel*, Vana Manasiadis takes this technique of paralleling and enacts it in the very form of the poems, by physically paralleling different sections of the sequences on facing pages. For example, a narrative poem/memoir/essay about, respectively, a past friendship or the time immediately after the death of the poet's mother, faces an ekphrastic poem about an artwork or text in 'Strata of Invisible Bodies' and 'Catalogue of 40 Days'. The reader may at first be a bit unsure about what to do with these separate pieces of the poem, how to reconcile them, what they mean together. But the human brain, being the pattern- and meaning-making machine that it is, inevitably looks for what those connections might be. One thing I think the poems are saying is about the way we 'read' everything through our experiences, our griefs, but also how art can act as a healing agent, to help us bear those experiences and griefs.

This idea is explored more in the poem 'Recommended Reading', which uses a different form of paralleling: the parallel texts are presented on the same page. The top part of the pages contain text about the books the narrator/poet is reading in the aftermath of her mother's death — 'So when Calasso said *The power of the abstract begins as a rejection of epic encyclopedism,* I could put away Mamá's medical files. When he said, *lógos transfixes in the merest atom of time what the rhapsodies had strung together and repeated over and over for night after smoky night,* I could get myself dressed'[8] — while the lower part of the pages/poem contain a narrative/memory of the mother trying to sneak her under-aged daughters into an R13 film. The two parallel portions act as a call and response, as referenced in the final lines of the poem: 'the chorus-lighthouse-compass pointing me to call response call response call//your call Mamá'.[9]

> I think there is a general misconception that you write poems because you 'have something to say.' I think, actually, that you write poems because you have something echoing around in the bone-dome of your skull that you cannot say. Poetry allows us to hold many related tangential notions in very close orbit around each other at the same time. The 'unsayable' thing at the centre of the poem becomes visible to the poet and reader in the same way that dark matter becomes visible to the astrophysicist. You can't see it, but by measure of its effect on the visible, it can become so precise a silhouette you can almost know it.
> — Rebecca Lindenberg[10]

Following perhaps the Montaigne-meandering style of essay poetry is Anna Jackson's long poem/chapbook *Dear Tombs, Dear Horizon.* She uses little fragments, often almost stream-of-consciousness, which range around her experiences while living in Menton, France, on the Katherine Mansfield Fellowship — what she sees, what she reads, what she's thinking about — a sort of poetic travel diary. In this kind of essay or poem/essay, to say that it is about any one single thing is to miss the point, but a recurring idea in the poem is finding new places to look back from — both literally — while walking in Menton: 'I walk up and down / impasses and traverses, looking for new / angles to look back from'[11] — and figuratively: 'literature does give us / another place to look back from'.[12]

Airini Beautrais's two most recent books both use the accretion of individual poems to build up an essay that looks at a topic from many different angles — also finding new angles to look back from. *Dear Neil Roberts*, through poems about anarchism, Beautrais's own history in activism, the 1980s and Neil Roberts himself, is an attempt to understand the life and death of this punk anarchist who blew himself up outside the Whanganui Police Computer Centre in 1982, six weeks before the author's birth. It uses lists, archival sources, news stories, conversations with witnesses, and doesn't come to neat conclusions. Beautrais's next collection is even more ambitious in its scope — in the poems that make up *Flow: Whanganui River Poems* she is responding to the Whanganui River, past and present, and the stories, mythology, meaning, cultural significance and people who belong to it. Poems as historical essay, poems as sociological study. In her dedication, Beautrais describes her work as 'an attempt at something like a collage or polyphony',[13] and says she felt 'a unified narrative was beyond my understanding and capability, and that a fragmented approach was better suited to the way I wanted to respond to local geography and history'.[14] This collage and polyphony makes way for many voices, many opinions, many angles.

> Poetry was an instrument for exploring the truth of things, as far as human beings can explore it, and it can do so with a greater verbal exactitude than prose can manage.
> — Thom Gunn[15]

'Poūkahangatus: An Essay about Indigenous Hair Dos and Don'ts', the title poem to Tayi Tibble's debut collection, is a sequence of prose poems that explore the ideas of hair, beauty and indigeneity; mixing memoir, myth, ancient history, recent New Zealand and specifically Māori history with pop culture and a splash of science. There's sass and humour, but also serious purpose: as indicated by the subtitle, the essaying nature of this poem is deliberate and conscious. The exploration is complicated and complex, and without simplistic conclusions.

Another poet who announces his work as an essay poem is J. T. Welsch in 'Effective Altruism: A Verse Essay', in which he explores the idea of effective altruism, with a parallel thread about *spoiler alert* the death of his sister. It uses a stricter form than many essay poems, with five sections of five five-line stanzas each. It reads as a conversation with a 'you', with his sister and with himself, as he struggles with how to deal with how one should live, which leads me to think again of those pre-Socratic philosopher poets, except Welsch doesn't posit any definite answers, despite all his thinking. Oh, but what beautiful thinking: 'what a privilege to make something of time spent / thinking all this to no end but the poem only you / are capable of writing'.[16] The poem is a satisfying and devastating combination of the deeply emotional and deeply intellectual — they never were opposites.

These few examples offer a somewhat haphazard and completely inexhaustive demonstration of what I mean when I talk about essay poems, though I am already regretful at my omissions, both local (Nina Powles, Helen Heath, Greg Kan, Lynn Jenner, etc.) and international (the genre-bending works of Maggie Nelson, the American lyrics of Claudia Rankine, and so many more). I hope in your reading of poetry you might start to notice this essaying, start to see it as another way of understanding a poem, and the essaying poem as a new way of understanding the world.

Here, at the end of this piece, it occurs to me that perhaps a constructive way to think about this convergence of poetry and essay in the essay poem/verse essay, is not to think of them as two genres meeting, but perhaps rather to think of poetry as the genre or form, and essay as the method. Essay as a verb rather than a noun. What a nice ending to this essay I thought this idea would be. But then my contrary mind had to look at it the other way: is essay the form, and poetry the method? Poetry as a verb? Let's poetry that. Yes, let's!

The language of poetry is a language of inquiry, not the language of a genre. It is that language in which a writer (or a reader) both perceives and is conscious of the perception.

— Lyn Hejinian[17]

1   Simone Weil, *Gravity and Grace* (Lincoln: University of Nebraska Press, 1997), 200.

2   Patricia Lockwood, 'How Do We Write Now?', *Tin House*, last revised 10 April 2018, tinhouse.com/how-do-we-write-now/.

3   Brian Dillon, *Essayism* (London: Fitzcarraldo Editions, 2017), 67.

4   Oxford Dictionaries, s.v. 'Essay', accessed 30 March 2019, en.oxforddictionaries.com/definition/essay.

5   Dillon, *Essayism*, 12.

6   Brian Blanchfield, *Proxies: Essays Near Knowing* (New York: Nightboat Books, 2016), 124.

7   Deborah Tall and John D'Agata, 'The Lyric Essay', *Seneca Review*, accessed 30 March 2019, www.hws.edu/senecareview/lyricessay.aspx.

8   Vana Manasiadis, *The Grief Almanac: A Sequel* (Wellington: Seraph Press, 2019), 95.

9   Ibid., 101.

10  Rebecca Lindenberg, 'A *McSweeney's* Books Q&A with Rebecca Lindenberg, Author of *Love, an Index*', *McSweeney's*, last revised 23 April 2013, www.mcsweeneys.net/articles/a-mcsweeneys-books-qa-with-rebecca-lindenberg-author-of-love-an-index.

11  Anna Jackson, *Dear Tombs, Dear Horizon* (Wellington: Seraph Press, 2017), 13.

12  Ibid., 9.

13  Airini Beautrais, *Flow: Whanganui River Poems* (Wellington: Victoria University Press, 2017), 14.

14  Ibid., 13.

15  Thom Gunn, *The Occasions of Poetry: Essays in Criticism and Autobiography* (London: Faber and Faber, 1982), 176.

16  J. T. Welsch, 'Effective Altruism: A Verse Essay', *The Honest Ulsterman*, last updated 1 June 2017, humag.co/features/effective-altruism.

17  Lyn Hejinian, *The Language of Inquiry* (Oakland: University of California Press, 2000), 3.

## Works cited

Airini Beautrais, *Dear Neil Roberts* (Wellington: Victoria University Press, 2014).

——, *Flow: Whanganui River Poems* (Wellington: Victoria University Press, 2017).

Brian Blanchfield, *Proxies: Essays Near Knowing* (New York: Nightboat Books, 2016).

Anne Carson, *The Albertine Workout* (New York: New Directions, 2014).

——, 'The Glass Essay', *Glass and God* (London: Jonathan Cape, 1998).

Brian Dillon, *Essayism* (London: Fitzcarraldo Editions, 2017).

Thom Gunn, *The Occasions of Poetry: Essays in Criticism and Autobiography* (London: Faber and Faber, 1982).

Lyn Hejinian, *The Language of Inquiry* (Oakland: University of California Press, 2000).

Anna Jackson, *Dear Tombs, Dear Horizon* (Wellington: Seraph Press, 2017).

Rebecca Lindenberg, 'A *McSweeney's* Books Q&A with Rebecca Lindenberg, Author of *Love, an Index*', *McSweeney's*, last revised 23 April 2013, www.mcsweeneys.net/articles/a-mcsweeneys-books-qa-with-rebecca-lindenberg-author-of-love-an-index.

Patricia Lockwood, 'How Do We Write Now?', *Tin House*, last revised 10 April 2018, tinhouse.com/how-do-we-write-now/.

Vana Manasiadis, *The Grief Almanac: A Sequel* (Wellington: Seraph Press, 2019).

Helen Rickerby, *Cinema* (Wellington: Mākaro Press, 2014).

——, *How to Live* (Auckland: Auckland University Press, 2019).

Deborah Tall and John D'Agata, 'The Lyric Essay', *Seneca Review*, accessed 30 March 2019, www.hws.edu/senecareview/lyricessay.aspx.

Tayi Tibble, *Poūkahangatus* (Wellington: Victoria University Press, 2018).

Simone Weil, *Gravity and Grace* (Lincoln: University of Nebraska Press, 1997).

J. T. Welsch, 'Effective Altruism: A Verse Essay', *The Honest Ulsterman*, last updated 1 June 2017, humag.co/features/effective-altruism.

Roger Steele

# On publishing poetry

Why publish poetry? This question is seldom far from my mind each time I stand up to launch a collection of poetry, and we've published hundreds of volumes over 20-plus years in the business. Well, not so much 'business' as obsession.

Sometimes I quote from the *Dead Poets Society* movie: 'We don't read and write poetry because it's cute. We read and write poetry because we are members of the human race. And the human race is filled with passion. And medicine, law, business, engineering, these are noble pursuits and necessary to sustain life. But poetry, beauty, romance, love, these are what we stay alive for.' Other times I mention the epigram 'Poetry is to prose as dancing is to walking', which also catches some of the magic for me.

Most commonly at launches, though, I credit skilled poets with mastering the hardest tasks in literature. If literature is a Christmas tree, they're up at the pointy end with the angels. They say the most with the fewest words; they make the ordinary extraordinary; they start with the personal and make it universal.

### Endings and beginnings

I became a publisher almost by accident. I was earning a perfectly good living in adult education in the mid-1990s, but happened to hear that Jacquie Baxter had a collection of poems that hadn't been snapped up by publishers. My own interest in them was initially tangential: I'd had a bit to do with James K. Baxter before he died in 1972, but knew nothing of his wife, and was simply curious to know what she had to say about it all. As I began reading her manuscript, James K. faded from my mind. Jacquie had her own stories and strengths, told with economy, directness and spirit. I became her publisher in a long and fruitful partnership.

Around the same time, I discovered that Hone Tuwhare had works mouldering in his leaky writing shed at Kākā Point, so I began shaping them into a volume. When Jacquie's *Dedications* (published under her nom de plume J. C. Sturm) and Hone's *Shape-Shifter* won national book awards, my fate was sealed.

Working with experienced authors is a privilege, and so too is working with writers on their first books. Few have made more impact in the past couple of decades than Glenn Colquhoun, after *The Art of Walking Upright* was named best first book of poetry at the national book awards. I am pleased to have helped bring Glenn's skills and perceptions — and particularly his message about the bicultural premise/promise of Aotearoa — into the light.

Glenn's second major collection, *Playing God*, was about medical matters, and spoke to doctors, nurses and patients in a way that few poets had, reaching vast new audiences. Books of poetry make an ideal gift: they link the soul of the giver to that of the recipient; they have more variety, fewer calories and last longer than a medley of chocolates; and they achieve all that for a cost seldom more than $20 or $30. This was certainly the case with *Playing God* and many more of Glenn's books we published. I would guess that two-thirds of purchases were by people who read it and thought, hell, I can't part with my copy, so I'll buy another for someone I care about.

### Introduction to poetry

Like many in the world of words, I blame one particular teacher at high school for lighting the fire that still burns in me for poetry. Bill Hendry was his name, a dashing man we nicknamed '007' after James Bond, but it was not Bill's macho qualities that impressed us so much as his clarity of thought and passion for literature. At high school in the 1960s we never got far beyond the basics like Shelley's 'Ozymandias' and Wordsworth's 'Westminster Bridge', but there was so much to like about those masterful sonnets. More personal was a poem that gave voice to my inchoate appreciation of beauty and distrust of militarism: Henry Reed's 'Naming of Parts'. During cadet training at school we had to learn to use a Bren gun killing machine, just like Reed's protagonist:

Today we have naming of parts. Yesterday,
We had daily cleaning. And tomorrow morning,
We shall have what to do after firing. But to-day,
Today we have naming of parts. Japonica
Glistens like coral in all of the neighbouring gardens,
And today we have naming of parts.

We touched on Whitman, and 'When I Heard the Learn'd Astronomer'
made a big impression. If there's a better eight-line explanation of the
mystique of poetry, I don't know it — although Tennyson's 'The Eagle'
achieves a lot in even fewer lines.

### Voices engrained in the land

Poets are so idiosyncratic it is unwise to group them, yet brevity insists.
I will begin, as Aotearoa began, with Māori voices.

Te reo Ingarihi (English) leans on the tradition of Shakespeare and
its innumerable fine writers. Aotearoa New Zealand has all that to
draw on and more, because in Māori oratory, haka and song is another
fathomless wellspring. I have space for just one example, related by
tohunga Wiremu Parker, who opened my young ears when he compared
the resonance of Shakespeare's 'To be or not to be' speech with a
construction often used in Māori farewells to the dead. Hamlet calls
death an undiscover'd country from whose bourn no traveller returns;
the poroporoaki, translated, enjoins the dead to go along the path that
thousands have taken, but from which no messenger returns. Death-
taking, breathtaking, rich expression.

We have enjoyed publishing many Māori voices, most recently Iona
Winter of Celtic and Waitaha descent. Iona's work is peppered with
words in te reo, so much so that even her kuputaka (glossary) almost
makes a poem itself. Poems by Māori writers often have layers of history
and confrontation not found elsewhere, such as J. C. Sturm's plangent
call to remember the lessons of Parihaka, or the ending of Rangi Faith's
'Conversation with a moahunter':

... How did it go, I asked.

Just one, he said.

Just one.

## Fine wine

I am compiling an anthology of poems about wine; it's going to be quite a seller, because the two are a partnership made in heaven. One of the great things about poets is that, like fine wine, many only improve with age. It's been a great thing to work with vintage exponents like Peter Bland and Kevin Ireland. I first read Peter's shrewd observations when I was a schoolboy in the sixties; sixty years on, his muse is as inspiring as ever, his craft as deft. Likewise, Kevin Ireland: 'weave a circle round him thrice, and close your eyes with holy dread' ... a living legend. Humour, gentle or wry, is never far from his poetry, the wit woven with wisdom and compassion.

## A note on editing

Can poetry be edited? In general, poets make the publisher's life easier than many other writers do, because they are ruthless self-editors and live or die by the maxim 'less is more'. In that sense they are more like sculptors than painters, whittling and chipping away extraneity from their block of wood or stone.

Yet I edit poetry as diplomatically (in my dreams) as I approach prose, and yes, it has challenged a few friendships. There are often words still to be trimmed, sometimes whole stanzas. Then there are 'echo' words, seldom found within a single poem, but repeated within a volume. One manuscript from a woman in her eighties had seven or eight references to bone or bones, each on its own apposite, but collectively it was hard to escape the osteoporosis lurking between the lines. Another poet, something of a swashbuckler, had *glisten* in one poem, *glitter* in the next, *glint* and *glister* on its heels and *glimmer* and *shimmer* following not far behind. Sparkling stuff, but, taken together, too much Las Vegas.

And imagery: if it's as stale as yesterday's pizza, it has to go to compost.

Just as novels need to be novel, so poetry has to be poetic: fresh, graceful, crisp, spare.

And not too raw, but reflected on, repaired, revised: Wordsworth didn't say it *all* when he talked about poems springing from 'emotion recollected in tranquillity', but he said a lot. In the same discourse he alluded to another key characteristic of successful poetry, that 'the verse will be read a hundred times where the prose is read once'. Poetry may be mysterious, but rewards repeated reading. Not that you have to 'get' it — who can really explain why they like a particular piece of music or other artwork? Rereading can reveal some new part of the poet's craft, but it doesn't matter so long as the effect pleases like the colours and shades of a painting, perhaps leaving a sense of intrigue or wonder. I still don't understand every aspect ('The heart that fed'?) of 'Ozymandias', and it's as beguiling as the first day its doors of perception were opened to me.

Talking about rawness, a word on *angst*. Every few days as publishers we are offered the angst-infested works of young people, but it's poetry as therapy and seldom ripe for publication. If there are words in it like *hurt* and *tears* and *pain*, it may be time to start again.

Many a good poet is a minimalist, so self-editing can include asking every adverb and adjective to justify itself or clear off. Similarly, the less punctuation the better, so long as meaning is not compromised or confused. And no, capitals are not needed at the start of every line.

**Poems on the page**

Once a writer has completed around 50 or 60 publishable pieces, the curation of a collection is the do-or-die next step. The more carefully poems are selected (or culled to 'mature'), organised and presented on the page, the more the collection will be treasured. Few are more adept at this part of the art than Siobhan Harvey. She has been the sensitive touch behind many an anthology, and her own first volume, *Lost Relatives*, was a paradigm. Its very title came from the two component sections she marshalled and manicured: *Lost* and *Relatives*.

When I lay out a poetry book, I try to have as much white space around each poem as I can, to let it breathe and stretch its arms. Some new poets try to achieve this by centring the lines on the page, but it has to be a singular work for this not to look amateurish. Left-aligned, with generous margins, works best. Two-page poems I always try to have on facing pages, so they can be apprehended all at once.

### Straw into gold

Poetry is straw, spun into words into gold. It can delve, delineate, uplift the soul of an individual or of many. It can be as superficial but as deceptive/effective as a cosmetic, or as deep and life-changing as open-heart surgery. It is music, painting, sculpture, theatre and dance all distilled into words arrayed on a page, but also nuanced in the gaps between words and lines. It is the things that can be said, and the things that cannot. For writer and reader, it is no easy taskmaster, but its rewards are everlasting.

Poets are the unacknowledged legislators of the world, said Shelley in a defence of poetry — not that it was under attack, then or now. Poetry is perhaps the most powerful and inspiring art form humans share. As children we are captivated by the rhythms of nursery rhymes. Soon we are soothed — or stimulated — by song, in which poetry is more often than not embedded. In our times of welcoming and farewelling we rely on the poetic passion of oratory, the quintessence of language. It has a place in every part in our lives. Poetry is who we are, and who we best can be.

# Reviews

# Heather Bauchop

Heather Bauchop
*Remembering A Place I've Never Been: The past in three voices*
Cold Hub Press, 2018
RRP $30, 104pp

The frustration of inheriting a partial family record, and with no possibility of filling the blanks because the stories have been taken to the grave, is the subject of the haunting debut poetry collection, *Remembering A Place I've Never Been: The past in three voices*, by Dunedin-based writer and public historian Heather Bauchop.

Made up of 81 poems, the book is arranged in three sections: *Home*, *History* and *Noone*. In the first section we are placed inside the mind of a man who has recently lost his father and who lives a long way from his family's country of origin. We encounter him in the midst of tracking through what he knows of his family's history. With only 'a sheaf of scraps / and sayings' to go on, and a handful of anonymous photographs, the poem 'His name' sets out the complexity of the man's inheritance:

> I have only
> his name.
>
> Beneath my feet
> someone else's earth —
>
> even if I found the place
> with standing stones and my name
>
> etched in granite certainty
> would that place be mine

or just the past looking ahead
with blind sight?

If I knew where I came from
could I be somewhere else?

An element of mystery creeps into the story when the man comes
across a document detailing the death by suicide of a female ancestor.
He identifies immediately with this woman, regarding her as a fellow
banished soul, and his mind sets to work stitching together a narrative
about her, fashioning a shroud of 'words formed / by my empty mouth'.
He invents a captivity narrative, with a dream of a white room with thick
walls and a small window, and then he offers her an escape by placing
her on a clifftop and imagining 'a woman considering / the gathering
clouds / before leaping'.

The process of invention continues in the second section where
the same man draws on his skills as an historian to imaginatively
reconstruct a late-nineteenth-century gentleman-farmer's residence.
It isn't clear whether this is his ancestral home, and the name of the
family, Noone, indicates that it doesn't really matter. Even with the aid
of the architectural plans and an old newspaper article describing the
interior of the dwelling, with its fine timber panelling, botanical-print
wallpaper, plaster-cast ceilings and marble mantelpieces, the blanks in
the Noone family story still remain.

The third section of the book travels even further with this idea when
the man discovers a notebook under a loose floorboard in a mysterious
white room at the rear of the house, with no handle on the inside of the
door and a bolt on the outside; a room that isn't present on the plans
of the house. The notebook, later catalogued among the Noone family
papers, is written by the daughter of the gentleman farmer whose young
wife died in childbirth.

We learn that her grief-stricken father shut the baby away in a locked
room where she was nurtured and educated by the kindly housekeeper,
Maude. The notebook describes her life in the white room, and the

notable occasion when she was discovered and befriended by the second young wife of the farmer, who had survived the loss of two unborn babies. Eventually she would meet the same fate as the first wife. And when her baby son was brought to the white room and placed in his half-sister's arms, presumably destined to live out his life as a fellow prisoner, the narrative suddenly circles back to the first section. We learn that it is she who has escaped and thrown herself off the cliff, and that the narrator's father was that baby boy, liberated by her act of defiance. At any rate, that's one possible story.

The first time I read *Remembering A Place I've Never Been* it seemed like a Charlotte Brontë novel that had been abridged to its barest essentials, but when I read it a second time I was more mindful that the rules of narrative need not apply because this is a book of poetry. In fact, they should be disregarded so that the larger point of the book can be revealed. To that end, I started thinking about the white room as a metaphor for the blanks in a family's history, the secrets kept and locked away, the facts abridged, manipulated, modified or diluted.

The details in Heather Bauchop's poems are so spare, however, that I found myself feeling a little desperate to know whether anything was actually true, so I started looking for clues. Firstly, I scrutinised the black-and-white photograph on the cover of the book. The photo credit tells us that the image comes from the archives of the Shetland Museum and that the building is the United Presbyterian Church and Manse in Ollaberry, a settlement on the main island of Shetland. Using a magnifying glass I tracked away from the bleak, boxy architecture of the manse, positioned squarely on a bare section with hedges on three sides, and up and over the brow of the hill where the spire of the church is just visible.

The magnifying glass allowed me to peer more closely at the blurred figure of a person standing on the step outside the front door of the manse. The figure appears to be a young girl with short dark hair cut in a bob. Her head is slightly bowed, as if she is reluctant to enter the building, or perhaps her stance is one of dejection following a telling-off and banishment to the front step. I started to wonder whether the girl in the photograph was the first person named by the author in her tantalising dedication: 'To Sheila May Christian Finlayson, the girl I never met.'

With only a name to go on, just like the protagonist in the collection, it wasn't hard to establish that Sheila May Christian Finlayson is (or was) the poet's mother, when I came across a notice in the *Shetland Times* from 16 August 1957 announcing her marriage to Thomas Bauchop 10 days before at Sevenoaks. Heather Bauchop fleshes out the story a little more in her biographical note on the back cover, describing her 'lost Scottish parents who migrated to Palmerston North via Aberdeen in 1972'.

The use of the word 'lost' to describe her parents is an interesting choice. It indicates that Heather Bauchop is the inheritor of this loss, and it seems that this is what the book is about. It is about the questions that inevitably arise when you are bequeathed holes, gaps, and a place that is completely foreign to you but is still connected to you. The poet describes this as an '[e]mpty inheritance' because you can speculate as much as you like about your family's history, but, ultimately, emptiness is all you will ever have and a sense of estrangement is all you will ever feel.

The photograph on the cover of the book amplifies the sense of alienation at the centre of Heather Bauchop's collection. The author's name, in white text, is situated on the outside of the fence marking the perimeter to the property, which I assume her family once lived in. She is positioned looking at the home that she can never enter in a place that she has never been, a point that the writer expresses simply and beautifully in the poem, 'Travails': 'Even as I see myself / sitting by the wall / I cannot cross. / My father took from me / this place / yet here I am'.

## Jenny Bornholdt

Jenny Bornholdt
*Lost and Somewhere Else*
Victoria University Press, 2019
RRP $25, 75pp

I know where Jenny Bornholdt got her poetry from: her grandmother. The opening and eponymous poem quotes Grandma disparaging someone's choice of outfit quite delightfully:

> Put something else on
> You look like a
> fun day animal.

There are so many 'fun day animals' in this book — by which I mean so many original and performative phrasings that capture feelings and observations afresh, most of them expressed with exuberant insouciance. It could be 'A day so full of promise / you might kiss your own arm' ('Storm') or autumn, coming 'clear and bold / as a Sydney waitress' ('Science'), Bornholdt just knows how to animate a scene. Or should I say Bornholdt can animate a scene like an episode of *The Simpsons* where Walt Whitman has a cameo? . . . Perhaps I should leave the cute descriptions to her.

Not all of the poems lift the spirits, though, and a number of them suggest the ways in which 'middle age / is one long goodbye' ('It Has Been a Long Time Since I Last Spoke to You, So Here I Am'). In these poems, people die, hawks swoop down on smaller birds, and nature is generally threatened. In 'Last Summer' two lost people are recalled. Two sentences follow, describing the place, then the people left behind:

A giant moon
drags the ocean in so high
they close the beach.
We lie at the centre
of night. Darkness
eyes us up.

Isn't this so evocative of the way in which the deaths of loved ones leave us bereft — seeing vacancy everywhere — and also threatened? It is also such a typically *Bornholdt* description, in that an epically vivid piece of figurative language — the moon hauling up the ocean as if he is a mythic figure reeling it in — is followed by a superb piece of vernacular, just in case we were wondering whether it was all right for us to connect with what was being said, whether it was still a poem for *us*, too — the ordinary folk.

There is much in this book about our own temporariness becoming a reality. It is a fact that is accepted without grudge. For example, in the poem 'Spring, Alexandra' the river is described as 'running like story / where everything matters / but all passes', and this sounds a lot like life itself. The last six lines of the poem are broken off into their own stanza, away from the greater part, which has been focused on the build-up to spring. In this last part of the poem, Bornholdt uses the simple ambiguity of the word 'gone' to allow our contemplation of what the scene will be like when the speaker and her partner have left it and the children continue playing in the spring, the summer, warmth. From there, if we wish, we may think about the scene as a microcosm of their lives, our lives:

Later, we hear children yell
as they swing out and let go
over the water. Again
and again they do this
until the light and we
are gone.

These lines are richly allusive. They describe young ones at play and perhaps two unrelated older people returning home. However, for me, they also gesture towards the longing for freedom and adventure that young people possess; the way in which parents have to let go of their children and watch them take risks and face challenges as they get older, how they step a back a little from their children's lives in order to leave space for development and autonomy — and then, they are gone. A huge amount of poignancy is loaded into six small lines.

But there are also haiku, and short, short poems. Sometimes accused of being a wordy poet who errs on the side of the prosey poem, Bornholdt really compresses her language in a couple of beautiful small poems. My favourites are 'Wellington Summer Haiku' and 'Once-tiny Boys'. I think, as I write this review, that the thing that makes me love Bornholdt's particular voice and style is her ability to evoke poignancy through humour. It is an especial gift, and one that all good sitcom writers swear by.

**Wellington Summer Haiku**
It is eight degrees
and the Thorndon outdoor pool
is swimming with leaves

In the Japanese sense of *wabi-sabi*, it is the perfect subject for a haiku. It is so imperfect, this pool all full of leaves, and so lonely, on this crisp day when no human being will join the leaves and swim. It is also rather funny, this shiveringly unappealing outdoor pool on this decidedly unsummery day.

Now, I refuse to quote the 'Once-tiny Boys' poem in full. You will have to buy the book for it. It contains the phrase 'armpit fart' and succeeds in being both hilarious and terribly sad. How she does it, I just don't know. It is wit and compassion distilled onto the page extremely clearly and concisely. It is, like the book as a whole, another bravura performance from one of our best poets.

## Janet Charman

Janet Charman
仁 *surrender*
Otago University Press, 2017
RRP $27.50, 120pp

Written as a response to her experiences as a visiting
resident at a Hong Kong writers' workshop in 2009, and as guest
reader in Taipei in 2014, Janet Charman's latest book is a neurotic and
increasingly funny document of the discomfitures of travel and cross-
cultural interactions. The settings — in and around low-budget literary
events — provide a useful backdrop for Charman's ruminations on
domesticity, gender and sexuality, since they are such prime ground for
awkward and self-conscious conversations.

The book begins with two scene-setting poems that juxtapose and
reassemble Charman's travel diary impressions, from details of her
setting up her room, to an awkward conversation about an invitation
for a massage, through to disjointed conversations about her work, as
well as various location markers: chopsticks, green tea, crispy duck,
soy sauce, tanghulu, The Cemetery of Confucius, The Peak Tram,
a man swimming naked in a reservoir. But it doesn't take long for
Charman's preoccupations with gender to take hold, and in a single
poem she manages to query a translation of a lesbian allusion in one of
her previous poems, note a man's dull remark on communication and
sex, imagine a couple in a quotidian marriage, observe the 'obeisance'
of women greeting a priest, and imagine the poet's equivalent of a
film extra giving the producer a blowjob for a shot at fame. Her self-
consciousness about femininity and middle age are also constants:
'eat an egg from an uncaged hen / my eggs are gone / so my cluckiness'
or '. . . culture warns me every everywhere / that in men's eyes /

i've entered my invisible years / at fifty-plus i am an object of no significance'.

At points, her more self-conscious feminist assertions seemed to me a bit strained and abstract, such as when she justifies her continued use of the cummingsesque lowercase 'i' by claiming capitalisation of the pronoun is an example of patriarchal hegemony ('whereas upper-case first person: / reads as the default generic setting / of uninterrupted male subjectivity / as neutral and universal in patriarchy / in relation to which / a woman artist / must perpetually distinguish herself').

But more often it is grounded in observation and experience, such as when she finds a potential friendship strained after critiquing a poem for its apparently transcendent ending in which a woman embraces 'her own silence to become her lover's inspiration'. The heart-breaking 'Wo de tian a!' is the standout. After visiting the much-advertised Che Kung Temple and seeing its colossal golden sculpture of the revered general, she goes in search of a female champion and discovers in the outer reaches of the Hong Kong heritage museum an installation on the famous entertainer Lydia Sum.

> ... every single frock makes me feel like a million dollars
> is the wrong equation for how we absorb the feminine
> since each piece is alive with jouissance
> then when i get back to the hotel i mention what i saw to one of the
> others
> and she tells me Lydia Sum was sometimes referred to as 'Fatty'
> affectionately
> and i want to burst into tears

Charman's sense of humour is mildly neurotic, self-deprecating and funniest when it builds on the cumulative absurdity of the situations she finds herself in, and her increasing anxiety around how she is being perceived. The strongest poem is 'some notes on shopping and present giving', in which she narrates her agonies over the politics of parting gifts to her various hosts and co-presenters. She decides before her trip to trawl the back streets of New Lynn for bargains, but finds little more than glass wetas, *Lord of the Rings* souvenirs and screen-printed tea towels, so opts to take 14 'moody and existentially drear' gallery exhibition cards she'd been given in 1990, reasoning that she will be able to buy cheap frames for them in China.

Once there, though, she wishes she'd gone for a simpler option, since she is 'crap at directions' and barely makes it to the Jusco shopping centre without suffering a panic attack. Back at her room, she assembles a sample in the plastic frame feeling 'like a forger', and agonises over the low-paid labour that is gone into their construction, the 'demonstrably negligible' dollar value of the gifts, whether pink cellophane will offend the males, or whether the cleaner will think she's an idiot when coming across the snipped-up raffia bows she's decided against. But it's the giving of the gifts that causes her the most anxiety.

> . . . two of the recipients separately said 'did you paint this?'
> i replied: 'i wish'
> and one of them laughed and repeated it 'i wish' as if that was a piece of
> idiom unfamiliar to him
> which made me feel clever again
> but in a non-painterly way
> only then i felt even more like a counterfeiter
> since i didn't invent that riposte i got it off television

There's an enormous range in this collection — it shifts easily from earnest socio-political theorising to haiku-style imagism, to sitcom funny. As a travelogue, it seems to make the point that wherever you go — or whatever role you're expected to play — there's no holiday from yourself. If anything, travel and cultural discombobulation can have the effect of amplifying your preoccupations and neuroses. Fortunately, Charman's are very engaging.

Allan Drew

## Nicola Easthope

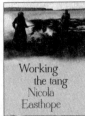

Nicola Easthope
*Working the Tang*
The Cuba Press, 2019
RRP $25, 87pp

I like this collection. Whether I come to *love* this collection, time will tell: although some poems in *Working the Tang* came straight at me, others took a path more askew, and will take time to absorb.

Easthope's endeavour is promoted by an examination of the multiple denotations and connotations of the word *Tang*, and this provides valuable scope for poetic riffs. The poems cover a great range of territory — 'from the Orkney Islands to the Coastlands shopping mall', as per the blurb — and a wide range of verse styles and poetic voices. If your sensibility turns to the lyrical, then you'll find some treats in here; if you prefer the direct and prosaic, then you'll also have happy moments. A bent for metre and music? — you, too, are welcomed.

This is a collection that strives to make personal moments have universal importance: this is, I think, at the heart of Easthope's work, even more than the variety and scope of the material. This happens whether these personal moments are hers (there is a strong sense of the poet's intimate presence in much of this collection) or if they're imagined of her ancestors. And she does this using both classic poetic techniques and with moments of innovation. There is the application of pure, vivid image: in 'Working the Tang, Birsay', a poem about the kelp industry in Orkney, she writes:

These women are wrapped for the weather.
The fleece of long-nosed black sheep
so knitted into their skin, when their men
undress them there is often a little blood

and you can't help but feel the threads of wool under your own skin, in a world cold enough that you have melded with your clothing. And then, you read the passage again and sense something in their undressing, too, that makes for blood in these women's lives. This image has a depth of both observation and compassion.

Easthope's human sensitivity is balanced with a perceptive eye for detail. In 'Morning' she describes a t-shirt in the breeze as 'corrugating in the draft', and upon reading it I felt there was perhaps no better way to describe and enliven this most mundane of things — those little moments of strange and unexpected beauty that might otherwise pass us by.

So much for lyrical beauty; Easthope is equally enthusiastic about making us cringe. Here's a passage from 'White pearls, hanging ears'

> but that sounds like a Maowri name!
> but you don't look it!
> and what about you?
> you have a Maowri name too!
> is that because you are part-
> or half- or did your parents
> have a special association
> with a particular native
> tree

It would be a rare New Zealander who wasn't transported in some way by this dialogue. And, God almighty, that terrible tension across the final line break: 'a particular native / tree'. I almost died.

Easthope wanders nonchalantly into intellectual territory, too. In 'Inane', she writes:

> When you say
> women don't earn
> the same rate of pay
> as men

because of the number
of absences due to
*monthly sickness*

does that mean
now that I am peri-menopausal
I will get a pay rise?

Moments like these in this collection provide, I think, relief from other moments in which the language is often dense and the meaning obscure. (If you are not educated in the genesis and background of each poem, you will probably not always know precisely what's going on — at least to start with.) This passage in 'Inane' is satisfying *in the moment*, like a fluffy macaron, for just this reason. It doesn't necessarily provide the longer-term sustenance that you'll take from poems that favour the perceptual over the conceptual. Nevertheless, the mere presence of this light prosaic relief indicates a poet with a great deal of concern for the wellbeing of her reader. The result is a strong connection, and much goodwill, between poet and audience.

Reading these poems, you'll feel Easthope in tight control of her craft. I have no hesitation in describing the writing as immaculate in its attention to detail and its skill. There are, I think, times when this control risks being overplayed. The innovation in lineation and the application of white space might feel, to some readers, contrived and distracting. On the other hand, these moments are absolutely not arbitrary, and if you take the time and pleasure to read these aloud you'll be rewarded. So, yes, I like this collection, and after writing about it, have come to like it more. *Working the Tang* is intensely personal but never shuts the reader out, and the variety is stimulating through to the last page.

## Murray Edmond

Murray Edmond
*Back Before You Know*
Compound Press, 2019
RRP $20, 74pp

*Back Before You Know* stands out from other New Zealand poetry books of the past year both in its physical and poetic forms. Physically it is a beautiful little book, appearing handmade and wrapped in card. Compound Press, who print and bind books in Auckland and say they 'maintain a particular though non-exclusive commitment to poetry of the Pacific Region while sea-levels still permit', obviously create books to be artworks in their construction as well as their content.

Poetically it is a collection of two poem-fables. The first, 'The Ballad of Jonas Bones', draws you deep into a style of long-form poetic story-telling so rare these days. It tells the tragic story of Jonas Bones, who likes to cheat and murder, a highwayman's nightmare in the colonial frontier lands of southwest Waikato. (It purposely plays on the form and story of American ballad, 'The Ballad of Billie Potts'.) Jonas's son, Rascal Bones, goes away (after some rascally business goes wrong). Having made his fortune he returns to celebrate with his parents, and a dramatic ending unfolds.

Murray Edmond mostly uses a variety of rhyming quatrains (typical of a ballad) in a clearly deliberate way, breaking form at times when the content dictates: for example, in a stanza that brings you forward in time (out of the ballad tale) the poem drops into free, unrhymed modern verse. He mixes these quatrains with speech and the odd couplet to create a story that roars along, and is an example of doing some *very-clever-poetic-things* while creating something readable and enjoyable, which I could happily hand to a poetry novice (or sceptic). This combination seems rare these days when Instagram poets rack up thousands of readers to the most basic of quatrains while literary poets take pride in how few people are able to comprehend (or be bothered to finish) their books. 'The Ballad of Jonas Bones' was first performed on stage in late 1984, and it will be interesting to see whether the printing of it revives any interest in performing it — you can certainly read it aloud to an audience of one.

The second poem-fable in the collection, 'The Fancier Pigeon', is very different in many ways. In this poem three interwoven characters share possession of a ring in a painful and intermittent love triangle which they can't all survive. This poem, although there is the odd rhyming verse, is told mostly in free verse, which suits the more modern timeframe of its events.

Though separate, the two poems are connected through the narrative of objects lost in water (which itself acts as a symbol for hiding truth), and through sea creatures who reveal these hidden things to us and the characters. In 'The Ballad of Jonas Bones', for example:

> Under the willows the eel's nose rises.
> The duck breaks from her enclave of water.
> Frog already in flight, back legs in limbo,
> but all that you see after the splash
> is the black hole of water
> as the jaws close over . . .

While in 'The Fancier Pigeon':

> Books in the library
> told her where the fishes went
> her study was to find out where
> those fishes hid
> with whom
> and when and where and even why . . .

Edmond has been a poet and writer as well as a thinker and critic in New Zealand for over 40 years. The poems in *Back Before You Know* have aspects of Edmond the poet, the playwright and the critic, and this book would be a great introduction to his work.

# John Geraets

John Geraets
*Everything's Something in Place: Writings 1980–2015*
Titus Books, 2019
RRP $42, 326pp

Let's begin with the disconcerting apostrophe in the title to this generously sized compendium of poems and critical essays. Is it an elision mark or a possessive? If the former, what is elided: 'has' or 'is'? Either way, what does the phrase portend? More, less or about the same as the cheesy 1970 Ray Stevens song about how 'everything is beautiful in its own way'? Or are we being given resigned counsel to accept what we have, since nothing has everything in place?

The title doesn't sound quite English. In his prefatory note Geraets refers to his 'direct engagement in Vipassana and Buddhist life principles', and some of his later poems draw on pilgrimages to India, Nepal and Sri Lanka. Is 'everything's something in place' a rough rendering of a near-untranslatable profundity from an Asian thinker — lifted, perhaps, from some text spied on the shelves of the Buddhist Publication Centre in Kandy?

The phrase appears again at the end of 'thirty7', one of several similarly numbered prose poems in Geraets's most recent collection, *Quite little ones* (2012), which begin by evoking a particular locale, then meditate on processes of cognition, language formation and poetry-making. 'thirty7' has the alternative heading 'anasuropa', a beautiful Pali term meaning 'absence of abruptness' — a more accurate way to describe moments of calm in a ceaselessly moving world, I believe, than the English equivalent 'stillness', which implies total immobility (a near impossible condition). Does a Pali-speaker habitually think in different ways from someone whose native tongue is English? Probably. Although we tend in our everyday lives to imagine we are in control of the words we select to describe our experiences, our choices are at least partly predetermined by how the language we use is structured.

The narrator of 'thirty7' and his companion or companions (the 'we' of the poem is left vague) are swimming at Taurarua/Judges Bay in Auckland's eastern suburbs while passenger and freight trains rumble past. The presence of locomotives prompts the narrator/Geraets to consider the persistent belief that our thoughts, like trains, are directional and have specific destinations. The railway analogy is soon rejected, however, as falsifying the fleeting, happenstance and unresolved nature of what, moment by moment, claims our attention. Perhaps our thought processes are more like immersion in an ocean or like digging in the sand for treasure. Geraets muses briefly on each possibility, then ends the poem like this: 'Most of what's dug up we discard. Why not use the analogy of a homely coloured bucket containing some sought after things that are scooped out or returned without fuss, like water or a train returning to station? Everything's something in place.'

And, even when given a context, those last four words, commonplace though they are, remain elusive, like a wonky axiom just beyond my grasp. Should they be treasured or discarded? The reader gets to decide. But then the same could be said of every phrase in every poetry book, couldn't it?

Geraets has always been a writer fascinated by the wayward, instantaneous workings of the mind, opposed to the shaping of our transitory impressions into tidy narratives, deeply suspicious of any conclusive wisdom, summarising epiphanies, pithy axioms. He's continually alert to the gaps that open up between the world, our perception of the world, our consciousness of that perception and the language that frames our consciousness.

Heady stuff then? A difficult read? Yes, definitely, but I don't want to suggest Geraets is always unsmilingly cerebral. As the mood takes him, he can also be playful, punning, whimsical, wistful, appreciative of sensuous pleasures. Underlying the thorny language poet is a keen-eyed and sensitive imagist. When he chooses, he's capable of work as tender and mellifluous as 'sweetcare', a sequence of love sonnets that pull off the difficult technical feat of appearing open-ended and free-flowing while abiding by a strict mathematical grid (not just 14 lines per poem but 10 syllables per line).

I confess that on my first reading of *Everything's Something in Place* I focused mostly on the essays. Curious about what Geraets had to say about Brasch's editing of *Landfall* (the subject of his doctoral thesis), Allen and Wystan Curnow, that vexing old fossicker Kendrick Smithyman, that neglected innovator Alan Loney, and Leigh Davis (Geraets's brilliant University of Auckland classmate), I raced through the poems, keen to return to the scintillating literary debates. But it's the poetry that has since lured me back for repeated re-readings. It's an intriguing body of work, so little commented on that it constitutes a kind of terra incognita, continually challenging but with something to beguile on every page.

I'll finish with a small example. Perplexed by passages in Geraets's 1995 collection *Sanage Adventure Field*, unsure of the 'design plan' (to use one of Geraets's own critical terms), I began pondering how I've now reached an age when I need a handrail to prevent myself from stumbling in the dark. Then my gaze alighted on these lines that seemed, teasingly, aimed right at me: 'the rail, keeping its distance down the stairwell. Fancy that, stare well.'

# Alison Glenny

Alison Glenny
*The Farewell Tourist*
Otago University Press, 2018
RRP $27.50, 80pp

Alison Glenny's first book is a fragmentary work which draws on her experiences on a field trip to the Ross Sea and Scott Base during her course in Antarctic Studies at the University of Canterbury. As winner of the Kathleen Grattan Poetry Award in 2017, the collection has already been widely reviewed for its form and aesthetic: it is 'rich in silence, enigma and erasure' (Paula Green), 'rich with precision, imagination and expansive relational observations of natural and cosmic forces' (Simone Kaho), and 'a ghostly outline of a larger story; an absence that casts a white shadow over everything' (essa ranapiri). But I'd like to add that its sparse textual form of blank pages, footnotes and erasures is less an aesthetic consideration than it is dictated by its underlying relationship narrative.

As Glenny pointed out in a recent interview with Paula Green on the collection, 'one of the things that appeals to me about the use of footnotes as primary text [. . .] is the invitation this seems to offer to readers to imagine their versions of what that missing primary text might be'. Call me Perez Hilton, but in accepting the invitation I don't see any ghostly enigma. It's pretty obvious the 'missing text' details Glenny's affair with a French photographer, cataloguing a miscellany of relationship details — some real, some imagined, many dreamed. Click for more.

First up, the content. The primary narrative recalls an unnamed 'he' and 'she' who meet and ultimately part again, revealing only fragmented memories of their encounter, along with letters and notes which the narrator seems unwilling to share except through hints and obfuscations.

> . . . Sometimes their
> fingers would touch during the examination of an object.
> The inevitable sparks were part of what he called *the*
> *magnetic process.*
> ('The Magnetic Process I')

She observes her lover with the same scientism that he applies to his study of the natural world, learning about his love of optics and nature, trying to absorb as much as she can of him before their inevitable parting.

> . . . Sometimes the moon shone
> through the thin curtains. It helped to fix his image in her
> mind, she said. Before a continent grew between them, and
> he could no longer resist its magnetic attraction.
> ('The Magnetic Process XI')

Before we are able to get too close to the lovers, though, the narrator begins retreating into the memory and the imagination. The memories are fragmentary, distant — literally footnotes to blank pages which convey a sense of paranoia — 'a feeling of heaviness', 'a feeling of being watched', and self-fragmentation arising from the need to bury the affair 'in the silence of the crevasses'.

> Études sur les glaciers. A pencilled note in the margin conveyed
> her sudden sense of being in the wrong place and the wrong time.
> 'As if I had been a part of something then abandoned.'
> ('Footnotes to a History of the Chryosphere, 1')

Secondly, form. As other reviewers have pointed out, Glenny's use of white space contributes to the overall characterisation of the environment — white pages do resemble the empty ice continent, after all. But while that might explain one or two poems, it would be gratuitous to structure the whole collection in that way if it weren't for a larger point. Given it is 2017, I think it is fair to assume that in rehashing postmodern narrative fragmentation — blank pages, poems consisting entirely of footnotes — Glenny is extending the well-trodden tropes of psychological fragmentation into a more contemporary post-irony. The redactions and blank spaces in the text reflect the tension between the lovers' circumstances, which force them to erase and conceal their relationship, and the writer's need to curate them into a compendium of experience.

> While leafing through the uncorrected pages she was surprised
> by their unexpected energy and force. This led to her attempts to
> reassemble the romance.
> ('Footnotes to a History of the Honeymoon, 4')

The remaining footnote-poems playfully fictionalise the affair through the story of a sickly Russian heroine who falls for an eccentric duke and explorer. But this relationship is fragmentary and doomed, too — ending in a farewell letter in which he regrets their 'continuous state of transformation'.

The final act is one of erasure. Letters between the lovers are presented in fragments, with words struck-through and brackets indicating missing text, as if the affair is so distant it is an *objet trouvé*. It is a fitting ending, given that at many points reading the collection is like peeking into a friend's illicit affair — you can't help but want to know the details, but get only fragments of truth. At its strongest points, though, reading the collection feels like having an affair yourself. The result is inevitably splintered, distant and uncomfortable — all in all, better forgotten. As such, the book ends with an apt erasure:

> You are twisted into my being
> [The remainder of the letter is missing]
> ('Correspondence')

Ted Jenner

# Michael Harlow

Michael Harlow
*The Moon in a Bowl of Water*
Otago University Press, 2019
RRP $27.50, 80pp

Prose poetry came to fruition in France in the mid-nineteenth century, and in the United States a century later. It is only just beginning to make an impact in this country, and possibly its most notable practitioner here is Michael Harlow. Harlow has been interested for at least 40 years in writing poetry in which the sentence rather than the line of verse drives the narrative, with its own rhythms enhanced by repetitions of phrase and image while making extensive use of those other familiar tropes of poetry, metaphor and symbol. His *Nothing but Switzerland and Lemonade* (1980) presented the reader with an often-startling array of sentences (many of them replete with surreal or Freudian images) placed one after the other without obvious connections of co-ordination or subordination, viz.:

> Today is the piano's birthday. Yesterday it was found weeping in the garden. Mother was not there, father was gone. But today is the piano's birthday.

That kind of parataxis has largely been replaced by the more conventional syntactical prose of narration in Harlow's latest volume, *The Moon in a Bowl of Water*. Gone, too, are the reader's worries about the apparently arbitrary nature of the imagery, which occasionally seemed designed to display the poet's ingenuity without being grounded in any individual human psyche. There is humanity in abundance in this, in my opinion, the most personal and accessible of all his books, grounded as it is in vivid personal memories and anecdotes.

We begin with acquaintances from the poet's early days in Greece and the United States, such as Miss Flora Florentine (described memorably as 'widow-thin and quick as a glistening whistle'), who snatches 'crazy' ideas like 'birds from the air' and vanishes, with a flourish worthy of the earlier 1980 book, into a novel by Anaïs Nin. And we meet an almost mythically Hellenic girl weaving at her loom (shades of Circe and Calypso) with such serenity 'that it was the light of herself that she was weaving'. These are basically happy portraits, bright with felicitous (in both senses of the word) imagery, which occur throughout the book. For example, the couple in 'A matinée special', who for strictly personal reasons missed their wedding and went to an old Fred Astaire and Ginger Rogers movie instead. And there's the old couple of 'Our ruby anniversary' who have saved their marriage by learning the value of out-talking each other.

Generally, however, the humour is either wry or grim. Among the belongings a sister leaves behind is an empty envelope addressed to her brother containing 'all the conversations we never had' ('Sister's keepsake box'). In the wonderfully ironic 'What is it a problem about?', Fred the 'skinny' hairdresser disappears into an urn of ashes which in turn goes missing, but Fred always wondered why people keep making themselves unhappy by trying so hard to be happy. In 'Think of that', a prisoner complains about the food and the freedom the prison cat enjoys now that he is reduced to a series of numbers: 'It's all body count, how they downsize the life we haven't got', a bitter sentence which illustrates the surprising new contexts Harlow finds for some of our clichéd turns of phrase.

One of the most striking poems in the volume is 'Rocking horse rider', which mixes gallows humour ('In a town where the heaviest traffic was at the cemetery') with a genuinely tragic family circumstance: a woman, who has lost her twin brother and whose love affairs have failed along with her faith in God, admits that her fate was, even so, to be nothing but the rocking horse rider of her nursery days. But the threnody reaches a peak in 'Counting backwards': 'our mother' narrates a tale of multiple deaths (premature and suicides), confessing that the hole in her heart that she was born with is 'still there'. Harlow's 1985 volume *Vlaminck's Tie* introduced us to the Jungian terms 'Eros' and 'Thanatos' (Love and Death), which, as is often the case with this poet, are not diametrical opposites so much as complementary concepts in a constant interplay whereby the one might be transformed into the other at any moment. 'The music of light-filled thought' is as fragile as the girl in 'Cloudy Sunday' who admits, 'I was carrying myself around like glass and I was very breakable'.

An engaging expression of this life–death (or light–dark) continuum is one of Harlow's many anecdotes received from 'a friend', in this case a peripatetic philosopher who has 'taken to calling his front foot *life*, and his back foot, *death*. Like being together and apart all at once' ('The weather in Mallorca and Tennessee'). Another poem, dedicated to the memory of Kurt Schwitters, focuses on the tense moment when the artist passes through a frontier post, allowing him to escape from the 'deranged' world of Nazi Germany and seek a new life offering him the freedom to 'dream of one day arriving *stous Delphous*' (i.e. at Delphi, site of the oracle of Apollo, the god of light, prophecy, music, and poetry).

Harlow orchestrates a variable line in his prose poetry, the length of which approximates to the pressure of the content or the emotion involved. There is a longer line for third-person narratives that move at a more leisurely pace, a shorter line for an excited first-person delivery. 'Little song on the Hit Parade' is set in couplets of alternating long and short lines; 'Fear of falling' almost drops down the page to its conclusion, 'there is nowhere else to fall'. Once again we have the usual repetition of pet phrases like 'instinct with elegy' (a reminder of just how frequently this tone/genre occurs in Harlow) and the reappearance of favourite images from previous books. The 'bird looking for a cage' recurs in a poetry in which words behave so often like birds (even 'nesting in boxes' in one poem in this volume). We revisit Switzerland and lemonade with Cézanne (in a parable about art), and Sappho returns in the dream of a woman disappointed in love *and* literature ('The gardeners').

Throughout the poems there are the usual Classical allusions, in phrases such as the Homeric 'three times blessed', and more obscurely in certain images: a photographer's 'black box camera' is described as 'the three-footed one with its darkness hood', which seems to allude to the third part of the Sphinx's conundrum in the Oedipus myth ('which creature walks on three legs in the evening?'). On the other hand, in 'That girl Persephone', the image of 'a dark-coloured bird cast in a hollow of snow' is working a little too hard, seemingly forced to double as the means of an annunciation of rebirth (Persephone's) *and* the ascension of the soul of the dead man who wanted to be carried out the front door 'feet first'.

Reading Harlow, you soon realise that he is not a poet of precise chiselled edges like William Carlos Williams or Marianne Moore. Events and personalities are sometimes muffled by obscurities of reference (his pronouns can be confusing in poems concerning family members). We are denied total clarity in the interests of the symbolic, the timeless, archetypal imagery that derives from our psychic heritage. The poem 'Counting backwards' contains quite an amount of autobiographical content which is not dwelt upon because the poet is more interested in the archetypal image of the mother's wound, her 'hole in the heart'. Rocking horses and more commonplace objects like walking sticks or a broom of willow twigs assume the almost transcendental significance of wands or golden boughs.

Not that the poetry reads as if it stems from the notebooks of someone who has been surfing the collective unconscious, but it does court an ambiguity of meaning and reference to a degree that is unusual in New Zealand poetry. The ambiguity comes essentially from his preference for the generic over the specific, for image and symbol over the literal. By taking such a risk when, as in this volume, he combines the anecdotal with a symbolist aesthetic, his poetry gains a depth and a universality that few poets in this country have ever achieved.

## Saradha Koirala

Saradha Koirala
*Photos of the Sky*
The Cuba Press, 2018
RRP $25, 58pp

The cover of *Photos of the Sky* is a rush of dreamy pastels, brushed on like watercolour. The cover matches Koirala's poetic style — light and dream-like — as she depicts the physical and emotional journey of moving somewhere new.

The collection is divided into four sections: *reach*, *shift*, *reach* again, and *this time*. Each section has a subtitle, the first one for *reach* being 'to stretch out to touch or grasp something'. This section seems to be a snapshot of Koirala before her relocation. As her biography in the book reveals, she now lives in Melbourne, and used to live in Wellington. Recognisable scenes from Wellington make an appearance: in 'At Midland Park', Koirala describes this park with familiarity. This green space lies in the middle of the city. It is surrounded by office buildings and populated with pigeons that she calls 'feathered thieves'. Koirala picks out a 'Man-in-suit' with a coffee cup, then a barista inside whom she calls a percussionist with 'crash-cymbal saucers'. In this way, Koirala wonderfully describes the bustle of Wellington city while also finding moments of pause in a simple park.

But moments of unease come out of the poems in this section. In 'On being solo', Koirala watches couples walk by and dreams of empty spaces being occupied. And in 'Mindful', Koirala finds herself being toppled by piles of paperwork. This unease hints at the change that is to come.

The second section, *shift*, is subtitled 'move or cause to move from one place to another'. And in *shift* a great change rumbling below Koirala's words echoes this meaning. In 'Bowie', Koirala's distress over

David Bowie's death becomes a thread to other moments of change in her life. 'David Bowie has died and I'm back to Valentine's Day 2004 leaping in Wellington rain', singing his songs. 'David Bowie has died,' she says again, 'and I buy potting mix to repot the succulent I decorated for Christmas', 'David Bowie has died . . . we listen to all our favourite songs of his, remembering all the other times we listened to those songs'. In this way, the poem brings the reader through Koirala's own personal history and its integral moments. Bowie and his music become anchors and landmarks for these shifting memories.

Like the first section, the third section of the collection is also titled *reach*. But in a beautiful play of words, this section means something else. The subtitle for this third section declares 'to arrive'. This kind of reach is different.

The first poem in this section is filled with longing, and immediately tells us that Koirala has reached her new place. In 'Nephew', Koirala softly writes, 'On the phone he points at things / I can't see from this country'. The great physical distance is encapsulated so efficiently, and when Koirala states that 'this welling in my heart will last days' it is an emotion that can be felt by the reader, too.

In the final section, Koirala's writing moves on from reaching and yearning into something more concrete and stable. This final section is titled *this time* with the subtitle 'eventually, at last'. This little subtitle feels like a breath of relief, suggesting that this is where Koirala finally makes it and reaches a point of comfort. Here, it is not just the landscape that Koirala becomes comfortable with. It is also the people.

My favourite poem in the collection, 'Balance', comes from this section. In this poem, Koirala talks to a someone, a 'you'. This 'you' is a person who is loaded with significance, and Koirala shows us this in subtle ways. She tells us that this 'you' is someone whom she can count on, and trust that 'of course you're not going to fall'.

In the poem 'This time', Koirala then describes events in her daily life. On Thursday, she walks in the sun even though she knows it can burn. She thinks, 'Walk through it, let it touch you . . . Sweat and burn. This life is all highlights and headlines'. Other events from other lives make an appearance. On Friday, a drowning boy's life is saved. On Saturday, someone visits their ex-partner in hospital. And finally, on Sunday, things are calmer. Koirala stays at home, but still she realises the frantic and unpredictable nature of any life. She ends the poem with her own description of life, stating that it is 'Highlights and headlines, imagined sunsets and a couple of tears'.

In *Photos of the Sky*, Koirala beautifully progresses through the changes and challenges that come with relocating. It not only involves familiarising yourself with the landscape, but also includes familiarising yourself with the people. She wonderfully portrays how the presence of someone familiar becomes a source of comfort, like taking a familiar route home. And as she describes snapshots of her new life, it is evident that she recognises how complicated and wonderful it can be. What was once just a city on a map is now a map of memories, both hers and others'. Some points on this map are tender, but they are all full of colour.

Elisabeth Kumar

## Wes Lee

Wes Lee
*Body, Remember*
Eyewear Publishing Ltd, 2017
RRP £6, 32pp

The world of poetry, a bit like the rest of the world, tends to uphold the idea that people (and perhaps especially women) who have been traumatised are welcome to keep it to themselves. The horror of abuse is bad enough; doubly horrific for the poetry-reading public to be asked to sit through it, with its mawkishly blurred literary boundaries. So *confessional*, so *therapeutic*, so well suited to the bottom drawer, or to somebody trained and properly compensated for having to hear it. So much better to be told slant, later on, in disguise, when the poet is ready — which is a way of saying that the experience of trauma should no longer be alive in the body.

If it must be told, the story of abuse should be told from the other side of a process of recovery or triumph. It should transcend, forgive, or move on. It should never feel like an excuse, it should look outside itself, it should reassure its readers without being pat or simplistic. It must find a perfect balance between wallow and skite, or what Jenny Bornholdt described as a 'ratio of crafting to blurting'.[1]

Wes Lee does none of these things. In a beautifully coherent cycle of 20 poems, she explores the memory of childhood violence in its bodily immediacy. Unembarrassed, she faces her trauma directly and speaks it aloud, inhabiting the poetic space without shame — evoking Margaret Cavendish's insight that 'all is not Poore, that hath not Golden Cloaths on, nor mad, which is out of Fashion'.[2] Lee's minute-by-minute physical reactions, the stuff that happens with breathing and muscles and skin, are never pathologised or pitied — instead we are invited to trust in their concrete, corporeal logic and bear witness, as the body does daily, to the terrible events that they index.

> In the morning we review
> what the triggers could have been:
> the girl half strangled on TV
> we glimpsed before I shut my eyes . . .

> *the players are dead,*
> *how dead they are,*
> *doorknob dead,*
> *dead*
> *dead*
> *dead*

Lee marvels at her body's prescient attunement to danger, and bewails its choice of action (why play dead rather than run? why disconnect rather than fight?). She draws attention to the way trauma folds time back on itself, the past existing as if for the first time in the present, always ready to happen again. In 'Body, you let me down' she describes the body's ability to interrupt her sleep with a scream 'so blood-curdling / I'm sure all the neighbours wake' — some to remember 'their own secrets buried'.

> Sometimes I stand and look at the lights in the valley,
> how long they take to snuff out,
> the poor children there wearing giant's bodies
> that betrayed them.

But the betrayal is not the fault of the body. Psychiatrist Judith Herman writes that a 'traumatic event challenges an ordinary person to become a theologian, a philosopher, and a jurist'.[3] Lee wields her vulnerability as an exhibit for the prosecution: 'The furniture / could not hide me / I had no weapons, / you bought the furniture'. In poems like 'Dolls' and

'Ka-Pow!' she catalogues the ways in which her abuser controlled every damaging detail, and calls down condemnation where it is roundly deserved. Language delicately teases apart the paradoxes — the adult still a child who wasn't to blame, the one who was made passive now a fiery protagonist, the deceased perpetrator still on the hook, the victim's experience somehow completely her own. The last thing Lee seems to want is for her suffering to disappear the way she was wiped from her mother's body, 'proud in a pinstripe pencil skirt / back to her original weight'.

In 'Poker', 'Find & Replace' and 'Search Engine', found fragments of awkward conversation and internet confession echo a profound sense of loss and isolation. Lee preserves the feeling carefully, honouring the blurt, exploring line space and compression in short, repetitive stanzas. In 'Reversals', she pares her explanation back to a whispered acknowledgement: 'I could only think or say some words backwards . . . The words were *esuba* and *cinap*'.

The C. P. Cavafy poem from which this collection and its final poem takes its title is a meditation on desire. Cavafy asks himself, as a body, to recognise the way he once reciprocated the glowing desires of his lovers, the way their longing now gains substance and lives on in its own energetic form. Lee gazes at her body and asks point-blank what it did with 'that part of me', crying out with a demanding desperation: 'Did you swallow it whole, you whale? / I feel it trying to sick itself up'. In the end, she imagines an act of protection and of transformation, an organic alchemy. Poetry, it seems, is just one of the places in which such suffering needs to be lifted up into the light, and the body do the rest.

---

1   Jenny Bornholdt, quoted in Siobhan Harvey and Liz March, *Words Chosen Carefully: New Zealand Writers in Discussion* (Auckland: Cape Catley, 2010), 57.

2   Margaret Cavendish, *Margaret Cavendish: Selected Poems*, ed. Michael Robbins (New York: New York Review Books, 2019), xiv.

3   Judith Herman, *Trauma and Recovery* (New York: Basic Books, 1997), 178.

# Owen Leeming

Owen Leeming
*Through Your Eyes: Poems early and late*
Cold Hub Press, 2018
RRP $19.95, 49pp

Owen Leeming's *Through Your Eyes* is a small chapbook with strong images. His last collection, *Venus is Setting*, was published back in 1972, the same year that he became the first recipient of the Katherine Mansfield Menton fellowship.

Leeming was born in Christchurch, although he has lived most of his life away from New Zealand. He eventually made his home in France, but there are echoes of New Zealand in his poems here. He describes the eponymous Wellington suburb in 'Oriental Bay', a poem that mentions the landmark Saint Gerard's Church and Monastery on the hill above the bay. The last few lines wonderfully present a seaside view: 'a beach of silence under the monastery walls, / while a ship slips anchor, disturbing the sea / everywhere, and a further word furrows into the sand'.

When Leeming travelled back to New Zealand in the mid-1980s, his French wife came with him. The poem 'Through Your Eyes', describes the experience of seeing New Zealand from her perspective. Leeming presents his wife's varied questions about New Zealand, one after the other: 'Where are the people? . . . Are the wingless birds / good for eating?'. He then describes all the things she loves about New Zealand: 'the absence / of human reverberation . . . You love my mother, and my brothers, lamb / cutlets, art friends in Kelburn'.

Many of these observations will have New Zealanders nodding in agreement; these are the same things they love. The final stanza is a loving touch, as Leeming tells his wife 'you are my love, strange love, / in that estranging country of myself'. In this way, the piece is a sweet insight into the oddities of New Zealand, from a viewpoint outside Leeming's own.

Leeming brings small moments of humour to his exploration of New Zealand. In 'The Cry of the Kiwi', he details the peculiarities of this little national treasure. In the first-person words of a kiwi, Leeming jokes that 'Some may class me fruit / or black and tan . . . a grocery'. The voice of Leeming's kiwi is proud — 'I am the big little bird / who calls in the Southern night' — but also timid, conveying the fears expected of an endangered species. The kiwi tells us that it still has many worries, despite the confidence it tries to show: 'great men with lights / tend also to unsettle me. / So I pipe uncertainly . . . Not do-do yet—ki-wi?' Even though the little kiwi's confidence is wavering at the end of the piece, it still wants to say its name with pride.

It must be said, however, that Leeming's style does not flow for the modern ear. An example of this is his poem 'Sirens', which references *The Odyssey* and brings up images familiar to classicists. And indeed, the poem reads like a grand epic poem. The sirens speak with imposing phrases, singing 'O outstanding X, / Ornament of your race, class, profession . . .'

There is a jaunty rhythm to Leeming's work, but there is a lack of excitement in the poems; the conventional writing makes the pieces feel outdated to me. What I love about contemporary New Zealand poetry is the way it can twist things of the past, and place them against modern values. It can explore what is traditionally revered and bring something new to the fore. And it does this with stanzas that split and morph, some with jagged edges, some that run on with a different kind of desperation. Leeming's poems are very traditional at heart, and I felt that I had read many like them before.

*Through Your Eyes* is a pleasant insight into Leeming's work and fills a gap in the publishing record given his inconstant presence in New Zealand literature. As Robert McLean tells us in his foreword, only a handful of Leeming's poems were published during the 1970s, and it was not until 2014 that two made their appearance in *Poetry New Zealand*. Leeming's exploration of familiar New Zealand places and images makes the collection a comforting read for New Zealanders, but in the landscape of poetry today, I would have loved more experimentation and a development in style and subject matter reflecting how much New Zealanders have grown, too.

Liz Breslin

# Mary McCallum

Mary McCallum
*XYZ of Happiness*
Mākaro Press, 2018
RRP $25, 67pp

That this collection is *XYZ of Happiness* and not ABC shows an attention to endings and to the happiness found among them. McCallum takes everyday happenings, things that can be overlooked as mundane, and gives them an element of spirit, of dignity. Conversational poetry, then, with an attention to the shapes of the words and language she uses, in an understated, unfussy way that draws the reader in to pay attention, too. As McCallum wrote in a piece for *Corpus*:

> One day, thinking about the book, thinking about Hat's family, I realised that *a father* is an anagram of 'fear' and 'hat'. Reductive, but true. *A father*, before Hat's sickness, had meant so much more than that. And another day in the shoebox working on her book it occurred to me that Hat used a few different names for her mother. I clicked on 'find' and did a check on the word itself: 'mother'. It popped up on its own, once. Then again. And again. And again. Not on its own but in another word: *chemotherapy*. Who knew? I stopped a minute and stared at the screen. Really? *Chemotherapy* had 'mother' inside it? And then I saw it — either side of 'mother' were the ghosts of the words 'key' and 'happy'. Which blew me quietly away.[1]

These realisations led to the poem 'C', the third in the collection. The 'Hat' referred to here is Harriet Rowland, whose blog became *The Book of Hat*, an early book from McCallum's own publishing company, Mākaro Press. But to the poem:

**1. WHAT TO SAY AFTER HER DIAGNOSIS**
This: *A father*
broken and re-
configured. To this:
*Fear. Hat.* Nothing left
over. Nothing to
spare after that.

'C', as mentioned, is the third of 26 poems — sorted alphabetically, with one poem for each letter from A to Z. 'A' for 'After reading Auden'. 'B' is 'Bee story'. She keeps this up through to 'Upolu', 'Vessels', 'we are shy hellebores', 'eXit', 'Yellow' and 'Zambia'. It is a neat device that could seem trite, but McCallum manages to avoid this.

'Vessels' is another poem of life against endings — a poem of not waving but drowning (à la Stevie Smith) set against a sea-view kitchen where 'my breathing boys / my chewing men' are busy being alive:

> They couldn't have
heard the splash or cry but saw perhaps
through the open window the failing

sun shining, as it had to, on white legs
in green water. Thought it a boy fallen
out of the sky. Something amazing. But
the sun shining on water can be anything

when you're tipped back swallowing milk
in an untidy corner with stacked dishes
and an empty cornflakes packet waiting for
your brother to recall the irreverent dance

moves of a cartoon Jesus.

Road trips ('Kikoi for sleeping in') and trips to the dump ('Love the glove') have common ground — objects of clothing infused with meaning through the practical tasks. 'Sycamore tree' has ampersands and a whirling aspect and a scattering of missed vowels and consonants that I can't quite pattern out.

'Things they don't tell you on Food TV' is a poem with zest, apt line breaks, rhymes and egg-cracking yolks, jumping off the page and taking you on a tasty frolic through McCallum's life in food:

come Easter in Crete

lambs are bloody sacks, milky mouths that
kiss the small of your back, and eggplant
is purpler when you call it aubergine, aubergine

is purpler when you call it melitzane, another
thing again when you call it Mellie-Jane, crack-
ing eggs is an act of belief whichever way

you look at it

It is hard to make it to the end of this poem without actually salivating just the tiniest bit, and with memory-bankers like this it is easy to see how *XYZ of Happiness* was one of the *New Zealand Listener*'s Top 100 Books of 2018.

The book is beautifully presented, with an iceberg on the cover that is also reminiscent of a happiness bowl:

it's in the colours of fire. Still angular, still
brimming. No equation on the glass.
It looks primordial
                    like a wedge
of something cut from a rock.

('Just happiness')

The inner cover is pink and reproduces poem 'P' — the evocative 'Pink T-shirt:'

> look through the keyhole
> to see the joy of her
>
> running down the stairs in a pink T-shirt
> cupping each large unruly breast
>
> not enough hands
> to stop the smile on her face.

Inside the inner cover, it is easy to suppose that the precise shade of yellow liaises with poem 'Y':

>                                                  I had to be
> on my mettle or you'd start again on what
> made yellow yellow as if that was the first
>
> rule of colour and I'd missed it. ...
>
>                 All the way home
>
> you couldn't stop talking — it was as clear as day,
> you'd at last found a colour you could live with.
>
> ('Yellow')

Within the covers, more stories of hospitals, compositions, homecomings and always those endings. *XYZ of Happiness* rewards recurrent reading, with its noticing and placement of words and happenings:

lightly, all
limbs, tender in the way
of tending, curious about
the invisible workings of living
things.

('Of trees')

It is this tender tending that makes this collection quietly extraordinary
— McCallum is on the mettle here, in just the right shade of yellow for
the occasion.

1   Mary McCallum, ' "XYZ of Happiness": C is for Harriet', *Corpus,* 9 July 2018, corpus.
nz/xyz-of-happiness-c-is-for-harriet/.

# Robert McLean

Robert McLean
*Figure and Ground: Poems 2012–2018*
Cold Hub Press, 2018
RRP $19.95, 51pp

*Figure and Ground,* Robert McLean's fifth collection, reminds me of when I was at school and I picked up one of those gilded hardback books of what poetry used to be like (except that this is a beautiful-to-touch sepia soft-covered chapbook). With its classical historical references and unironic use of words and phrases like 'The Passion', 'provenance', 'perturbation', 'erstwhile' and 'libations', it seems far outside the current New Zealand poetic mould.

'Anachronism never pleases,' McLean writes in 'A View of the Canterbury Plains'. And I, for the most part, agree.

The people I felt I might have to look up to understand this book better are Tarkovsky, Walker Evans, James Agee, Jacopo, Giardino, Alberti, Walter Landor, Alfred Agostinelli, Richard Avedon, Schliemann. People I didn't have to look up: Anne Sexton, W. G. Sebald, Colin McCahon, Dan Davin, Napoleon. People I looked up to check I didn't have to look them up: Geoffrey Hill.

I resisted looking up the first list, wanting the poems in themselves to be the worlds by which I understood them. I think McLean wanted this, too, if we are to trust the ethos expressed in 'Against invention':

> May lack compel
> we fuller and substantive parties
> who bear the blood if not name
> of our mum's dads to flesh out men in
> verse and prose, perhaps reclaim

the diffident past, indict in art these
ghosts measured against invention.

Alberti, I think, may be gutted that his good art is being supported by
bad money. Alfred, I think, is unrequiting:

> Paris becomes you. Farewell
> you silly man — I gave you what I chose
>   to give, but what, no one else knows,
> Yet in the end,
> to me, you only ever were a friend —
>   but love is love, my dear Marcel.

('Le Petit Testament d'Alfred Agostinelli')

And Napoleon, I think, has fictionally found himself in New Orleans:

> I haven't seen France for thirty years.
>   But at least British Sea Power
> Didn't once again carry the hour.
> The *Méduse* caught it unawares.
>
> I sailed to the United States
> and reconstituted myself
> *sans* privilege, power, or wealth.
> Talleyrand and his ilk weigh our fates.

('Napoleon in New Orleans')

French words are smattered through McLean's poems like libations
of tomato sauce on hot chips. Actually, no. They're not as jarring as a
ketchup libation. And ketchup is too modern to make a showing. So in
the world of his poems, they work. Perhaps this absolute lack of modern
reference is what makes this collection hard to hook into, much as I
appreciate the craft.

Here's how McLean describes his formalism:

In short, I utilise non-organic form(s) for extra-poetic ends. Mediating
reconciliations between sincerity of utterance and pre-determined
patterns of relationship is utopian i.e. political. The integrity of every
syllable is constitutive of structure, which is in turn dependent
on maintaining the former to remain legitimate. To do so without
semantic violence intimates my hope correlative social and inter-
personal resolutions can also be possible. After all, the word is no less
indeterminate or relative than the human.[1]

I agree that every word, and every syllable therein, is important, in its
place, in a poem. But to me, the essence, the necessity of a poem can get
strangled if the structure is too strongly scaffolded.

As to the rhyming, sometimes it seems that the words have been bent
to the will of exact sonic association. Read this one aloud to get your
tongue and ears around it:

**Indexes & Libations**
(in memory of Dan Davin)

Our maple tree's in bloom,
sap quickened in its branches.
A tui cries; another answers.
Sunlight floods our living room.

Poems about El Alamein
lie strewn across the floor,
the yield of one man's war
focussed by age and pain.

His battle lasted forty years.
Love proved not enough

to outweigh that bloody stuff.
Death left life in arrears.

Now we set his life in order —
this poem after that poem,
knowing that we cannot know him
Is this what he fought for?

Days lengthen towards spring,
but it's winter nonetheless.
We forage for watercress
and talk of other things.

'Watercress/nonetheless' is an excellent rhyme, but, jarred by its very neatness and questioning its plausibility, I fall down an internet hole — *Dan Davin, watercress. Must include 'watercress'.*

*Figure and Ground* was on the *New Zealand Listener's* Top 100 Books of 2018, which is one reason to persevere with it. Another: it is so different from most of the poetry collections that cross or forge paths these days. McLean stakes that ground. In a 2015 review, he marks his own views on the current state of New Zealand poetry, deriding 'another book of dream-associative family reveries . . . the go-to for middle-of-the-road New Zealand poetry'.[2] With its staunch classicism and patriarchal worldview, *Figure and Ground* falls/rises/sits about as far away from that category as is possible, anachronism and all.

---

1   Tim Jones, 'An Interview with Robert McLean', *Tim Jones: Books in Trees,* 4 March 2010, timjonesbooks.blogspot.com/2010/03/interview-with-robert-mclean.html.

2   Robert McLean, 'A Make-shift Shelter of In-flight Magazines' *Landfall Review Online,* 1 November 2015, landfallreview.com/a-make-shift-shelter-of-in-flight-magazines/#more-2704

Jack Ross

# Cilla McQueen

Cilla McQueen
*Poeta: Selected and new poems*
Otago University Press, 2018
RRP $39.95, 296pp

Cilla McQueen's *Poeta* is a kind of collected/selected
poems, together with some new work. It spans almost 40 years of
published poetry, and no doubt some years of practice before that. She
herself is clear on her intentions for the collection, specifying that:

> These poems have been grouped . . . in rooms, where they have had a
> chance to converse, being related in my mind to one or another of my
> preoccupations as a poet. Arranged as a span rather than as a time-
> line, the sequence remains roughly chronological, with idiosyncratic
> exceptions.

One very useful convention she has adopted is the inclusion of 'the date
of first book publication or, where poems have not previously appeared
in a book the date of composition' at the end of each poem.

This is one of those brilliantly simple ideas which are so immensely
helpful to scholars and common readers alike — a little like the device
of including the date and age of the subject on each page of a biography
— that it's difficult to understand why *everyone* doesn't do that.

The point about the rooms seems a useful one, too. When I think
of McQueen's poems, I think first of meeting her at her house in Bluff
during a 2006 poetry symposium, mainly because I'd had to send down
some books for the occasion and hers was the only fixed postal address
the organisers could muster.

I remember the slightly bemused courtesy with which she accepted
this commission and greeted this comparative stranger, and the

amusement with which she regarded each new invasion of poets on their way up the hill to the marae: rooms, yes — beautifully composed and uncluttered rooms, with their harvest of paintings and books from her many years at the centre of so much of the creative life of the region she lives in.

I have to confess to having had some doubts about McQueen's last substantive book, her poetic memoir *In a Slant Light* (2016). Its reticence puzzled me somewhat, as I said at the time. I'm glad to say that this is not the case with this wonderful new collection. There has never been any doubt that McQueen is supremely adept at the complex, many-layered lyric, and this is the best place to find the very best of them.

More to the point, however, the extracts from *In a Slant Light* included here seem to me to work very well *as lyrics* — or lyrical narrative excerpts, if you prefer. I guess I was too busy reading it *as* a memoir, and so failed to see that it was actually just an adjunct to this many-roomed mansion that she has been constructing so carefully over the years.

What are the particular highpoints, for me? Well, I'll never stop loving 'Homing in' and 'Timepiece,' but then *they* can be found in anthologies — and even in the memoir itself. What was most exciting about reading through this new collection (and it really *does* make a difference that her publishers have given her a wonderfully resilient hardback to hold these nearly 300 pages of poems) were the unexpected gems, which I should have known already, but in many cases didn't. Poems such as 'Kids on the Road', for instance:

> you know, I would like to kick
> t.s. eliot in the head
> because you shouldn't have to pass
> english exams to love poetry

I like particularly that conspiratorial 'you know' at the head of that passage. How many of us have felt similarly oppressed by some such

GOM (Grand Old Man) or GOD (Grand Old Dame) of poetry? They may have been wild themselves once — perhaps are wild still — but not in the embalmed form with which we are forced to unwrap them from their mummy bandages in some dreary classroom.

The poem continues:

> no more puzzles for clever sleuths
> I'd just like to
> smile at you broadly
> and hand you the whole world
> clean on a plate.

You'd have to be pretty jaundiced to resist the charm of *that*.

I did feel — at the time of reading her memoir — that there was a strong contrast between the seeming simplicity (and actual cunning) of this early lyric voice that might have been vitiated by the many, many poetic experiments — collaborations with artists, captions to photographs, travel poems — she's conducted over the years.

When one reads such a late poem as 'Epitaph', however, such fears dissolve:

> Alas shall I in time become
> of all no more a part than stone
> or blackbird drumming up a worm
>
> And what can worm say in a poem
> but dark loam and the sound of rain?

The breathless, run-on diction here puts one a little in mind of Stevie Smith, but a Stevie Smith far less assertive of her own idiosyncrasies. The substance of the poem recalls Wordsworth, I suppose, and (a little) John Clare.

But saying that says little about the poem itself. McQueen has learnt from her lifetime's work to be supremely herself — reminiscent of other poets at times, as all great and consummate writers are — but instantly recognisable as having been inspired by *things* and *experiences*, not simple delving in books:

> I remember the look
> of the unreadable page
>
> the difficult jumble
>
> and then the page
> became transparent
>
> and then the page
> ceased to exist:
>
> at last I was riding this bicycle
> all by myself.

It would be easy to illustrate — for any sceptics still left out there — the complexity and subtlety of McQueen's thought, as embodied in these many, many glass cages of words — but, like her, I think it's better to go on 'stopping for shivers / woggly trees in puddles / . . . a coin on the road / a rusty key'.

This is a beautiful book by a wonderful poet.

## Michael Morrissey

Michael Morrissey
*Poems from Hotel Middlemore*
Cold Hub Press, 2018
RRP $19.50, 37pp

Michael Morrissey's latest poetry collection centres on a question: what does it mean to be mentally unwell? *Poems from Hotel Middlemore* approaches this issue from a range of angles, drawing on personal histories, philosophies and purer observations, and yet holds back from drawing any conclusions.

If one of the goals of poetry is to comfort the uncomfortable and discomfit the comfortable, then this collection sits squarely in that zone. Morrissey generously calls on what we can't help but feel are his first-hand experiences in the mental health system to populate his poems. In 'My mother thought atomic bombs affected the weather', the poet traces the experience of being pulled along by a delusional parent as she seeks both escape and help. It's the particularity of the experiences and images that set up both this poem and the collection as a whole.

The mother, believing all food is drugged, 'cracked open an egg in a phone box / and emptied the yolk into her mouth'; when he is taken to boarding school he is bathed by other boys in 'water grey and speckled with hairs'; the 'purple-threaded noses' of the men in the park are vivid and haunting. Moments like these stay with you after you have put the work down. While we might not be able to relate directly to each of the experiences in the poem, they are nonetheless evocative of one man's perception of reality: in their understated terror, these images are comforting.

Morrissey's honesty and generosity of voice, and the undeniable importance of the material, is not always matched by precision in some aspects of craft. Diction is at times a strength, at others a weakness. He leans on words like 'mad', 'crazy', 'lunatic' and 'looney' a little too often, even if he uses them with heavy doses of irony. Application of figures of speech, too, vary across the poems. Every now and again we come across a simile that doesn't seem to fit. In 'I'm crazy and I can prove it' the comparison of mania to the exhilaration of 'a Saturn V liftoff' feels forced; in 'At the hearing for my sanity', the simile 'social intercourse is as dangerous as forked lightning' feels a bit tired; and in 'Morning becomes electric', the description of Valerie's face as being 'bukkaked with tears / ejaculated from her eyes' is unhelpfully vulgar. On the other hand, the line 'birds like lazy shrapnel' is both startling and difficult — complex, fraught and hard to visualise — in other words, entirely appropriate for this material. Likewise, when the poet says 'Aziz and I clasp hands / an esperanto of fingers' there is a similar sense of complexity as well as connection.

The most useful and interesting imagery in the collection is the extended metaphor in which psychiatrists are repeatedly compared to the Pope. This metaphor runs throughout the collection. The comparison is open enough, and interesting enough, that it provides a compelling thread and allows for a kind of narrative progression. It also facilitates riffs on religion and cosmology, and Morrisey is not shy to invoke God, the Devil, Mary, the messiah, the universe, stars and planets to develop his ideas. And yet, again, as with other aspects of this collection, the Pope metaphor risks being overplayed, and in many poems Morrissey repeats himself by criticising the Pope-esque infallibility of the psychiatrists. The point is an interesting one, but its effectiveness is diminished with each repetition of the same idea.

It is hard not to love Morrissey's observations about golf in this collection. As I said above, he's interested in the question of what it means to be mentally unwell. In 'The insanity of golf' he makes an important point about how the distinction between wellness and illness can be a matter of point of view: 'considered rationally,' the poet says, 'what could be more irrational / than trying to sink a ball the size / of a giant albino testicle / into a hole the size of a can of beans?'

Golf is merely 'a frivolous use of lawn / the grass softer than a lunatic's eyebrows'.

The poetic voice is ironic, and at times almost sardonic. In 'Unwell', Morrissey writes 'God made a mistake in creating the devil / but psychiatrists are infallible / they have out-poped the Pope / comforting to know human beings / are higher than God'. These moments are satisfying in some ways: after all, who doesn't enjoy pointing a judgemental finger at the power structures that affect and control you? However, these moments also feel defensive. His approach to voice works best, poetically, when it leads to more honest and vulnerable lines — which is exactly what happens in 'Unwell'. The poem finishes with the observation that 'something the psychiatrists never do / they never leave you alone'. This is the heart of the matter, and expresses a longing for autonomy and agency in a world that will repeatedly and heartlessly deny you this. And, by the end, the collection is interesting, funny, honest, and irreverent enough to recommend itself to any reader with compassion.

Elisabeth Kumar

## Robin Peace

Robin Peace
*A Passage of Yellow Red Birds*
Submarine Poetry, Mākaro Press, 2018
RRP $25, 79pp

This debut collection, beautifully presented by Submarine of Mākaro Press, was born out of a hundred-day poetry-writing challenge, and dedicated to Peace's mother, who died in 2016 at the age of 93. Like her mother, Robin Peace is devoted to place — to exploring, cataloguing and sustaining it.

The collection, fairly substantial in length, is loosely arranged like a sampler, or perhaps an odds-and-ends drawer — 'collection' seems the right word, each of the 50 poems holding a memory or a question with varying degrees of polish. The poet's attention is caught by a glittering array of things: an unusual word, a feeling of dread, a slippage of meaning. Some of the poems are prompted quite arbitrarily, others nudged into existence by world events. Much of the work seems to comment on the way that such an exercise shapes the poet herself. What itch, exactly, is scratched by these brief acts of expression?

> I ask for a word a day. You lob me
> 'forest' and 'simple' and 'depth'—
> in a loose, uncounted moment,
> 'rain over the pond'. . .
>
> So I stop asking for words.
> Faced with the impossible, I seek
> St Francis with his arms upraised
> releasing birds into a changeling sky.

The collection also deals with race, the uncomfortable inheritances of whiteness, and the experience of feeling at home in a strange — or a stranger's — land. In 'The placing of parts', Peace offers a tender European pepeha, while elsewhere she nestles into a difficult in-between: 'I / am / the alien / outside'.

Although this book is not presented as solely a treatment of bereavement, or even the wider narratives of ancestry and place and all the disruptions they inherit, it is profoundly shaped by all of these familial forces. In those moments that stop all the clocks, Peace pauses, too, and surveys the geography of grief and loss and threat — this from 'Absence':

> I have not tackled the absence.
> Anchors and fishes scaling
> the bowsides are catchy
> reminders, but not enough.
>
> The anchor of absence
> tackles the fishy reminder
> that you have scaled away
> and been caught up.

These poems are rich with allusion, echoing folk songs and Foucault, but Peace's gaze is drawn to the empty places, those that nobody talks about. In 'Death inn', she looks in vain for a poetic description of death that captures how long it takes: 'But of the waiting / there is no word'. Of course, part of the reason we each seem to look afresh for those descriptions is that they fade so quickly, are so inevitably filled or covered over unless we pay careful ecological attention to their preservation. 'There are gaps in my days now,' Peace writes in 'New silence', 'where the words / shut their mouths', and even those empty spaces are fruitful ground.

Johanna Emeney

## essa may ranapiri

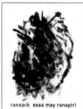

essa may ranapiri
*ransack*
Victoria University Press, 2019
RRP $25, 96pp

Punctuated by letters to Virginia Woolf's Orlando, which both confide and seek reassurance, *ransack* is a collection that wrangles with the meaning of meaning-making itself, particularly in the context of gender identity.

Where Orlando appeared to morph easily from man to woman in Woolf's satire, the speaker of these poems (I interpret the speaker as the same persona across those poems and letters that have i/I-speakers) has to fight and be exhausted just to inhabit the body they know should be theirs. Accordingly, poems of dysphoria situate the reader right at the fast-beating heart of it, where the speaker wonders whether to cut into their skin, 'consider[s] taking it off' ('Slice through thigh skin because people can't see thigh skin') and then contemplates just ignoring the penis, 'that meat alien', as if lack of attention might make it wilt away to nothing:

> like a flower I once kept as a kid
> that died
> when I stopped noticing it ('detachment')

A letter to Orlando describes the speaker's nightmares of an endlessly regenerating fanged snake/organ swallowing them, and ends with the confession: 'Orlando I never stand up when using the toilet and *he* is like a bumblebee stinger on my tongue when I say it'.

In 'she cut her face shaving', the forward-slashes do violence to the poem, underscoring the painful mismatch of reflection and reality.

The jagged lines of the poem, too, emphasise the exercise — its physical aspect and its jarring nature as an act carried out on this face given the 'she' of the title. Twenty years spent in an ill-fitting form, and at last she is going to work as herself — yet there is the reminder of having to do away with the facial hair, that necessary but incongruous morning ritual:

> the smeared blood / flat down caught
> over creases in the neck / the base
> of the chin / the pencil skirt / the
>   short / cut / the hair / the straight
>    lines of the jaw / that testosterone
>   bought her / the droplets glistening / about
>   her adam's apple / quivering to the beat
>     of her / lateness / twenty years
>    late to work in / the morning

Despite the very frequent engagement of the poet with aspects of non binary life that are awkward, uncomfortable and painful, there are gorgeous softnesses in this collection, too, where the reader can feel moments of self-acceptance flash into the speaker's consciousness. When that happens, the mood lifts and brightens. The poem 'the sparkle in ur eyes versus my dysphoria' addresses a friend or lover who paints the speaker's nails lovingly with silver varnish and is luminous in its acknowledgement of how kindness can bring contentment and ease. This act appears to remind the speaker of the place they wish to inhabit, which is not just one of femininity and calm, but also one of acceptance and love. The last four lines turn the whole poem around.

> shaking hands
> are covered in fur like some
> ghastly orang-utan
> was grafted into my being at the age

of thirteen
the largeness and the wrinkling skin
makes my mind into a ghost
and body into
a material reaction
the stomach bunches and folds like
white meat
u blow on my fingers
and I feel ur breath in the
soft gaps
that I am trying to live in

Another poem that hinges on the tactile sense, using tense and touch to change the mood suddenly, is 'canine', in which the speaker admits 'I never could pat a dog without feeling like my touch might hurt it'. The poem ends with the speaker's hand in the dog's fur: 'I can feel the whole thing moving in tiny ways. I feel moved in so many tiny ways'. Throughout the collection, touch is a reminder of existing and loving. In 'a phone call about the nature of pronouns gendered and otherwise', even when physical intimacy is not actually described, the fact of wanting someone is conveyed with a metaphor of physical touch. The persona is talking with someone about pronouns for nonbinary individuals, and which one is most appropriate for the speaker, who, now, confides (perhaps to the readers more than to 'u', the person on the other end of the phone who so understands them) that they are:

wishing u were mine
listening to the clap of ur feet
as ur
walking home or to a friend's house
it is raining in the dark

u push my name against the things i tell u
and that feels important

What a great couple of lines: 'u push my name against the things I tell u / and that feels important'. It is so corporeal, and it magnifies the way in which the person on the phone makes the persona feel listened to, valued and, I think, loved.

I have read collections that have had epistolary elements. I have read collections that have transported famous fictional characters into their pages. essa may ranapiri makes the letters to Orlando seem quite organic and unforced. They are not self-conscious or intellectualising. They come across as heartfelt confidences. In fact, *ransack* as a whole gives that impression: it is an intimate book.

This is an honest, interesting collection with a voice that is both vulnerable and arresting. Many of the poems are innovative in their structure and style. With every rereading I felt as though I was learning something and feeling something.

## Vaughan Rapatahana (editor)

Vaughan Rapatahana (editor)
*Ngā Kupu Waikato: An anthology of Waikato poetry*
Waikato Press, 2019
RRP $15, 96pp

When the great Australian poet Les Murray visited
New Zealand in 1988, I interviewed him for *Landfall*. Knowing he was
based in the small settlement of Bunyah (population 140) in rural New
South Wales, I asked a gauche question about pursuing a literary career
away from the main centres. He replied that we live on a globe and any
point on its surface is as central as any other.

Murray's retort often came to mind as I read Rapatahana's excellent
anthology. A similar point of view informs one of my favourite
contributions, Maris O'Rourke's 'Friday night in Te Kuiti', in which King
Country attractions are compared to global icons: 'like Las Vegas', 'like
the Champs Elysees', 'like gelato in Rome', etc. In her author's note,
O'Rourke describes herself, delightfully, as a 'peregrina', so when she
says the steak-and-mushroom variety from the pie-cart outside the
railway station on Rora Street tastes as good as 'a Michelin five-star
meal' (especially to a woman used to doing all the cooking herself), who
the hell am I to argue? What I most admire about this poem, however,
is how, through a skilful selection of vignettes, O'Rourke manages to
suggest not only an entire life, but a life as rich as any on the planet.

*Ngā Kupu Waikato* ends with several collaborative works, including
tanka sequences that involve six different authors. Even before this,
however, the anthology has an unusually choral feel, largely due, I
suspect, to Rapatahana's quiet skill as an arranger and conductor of
the choir. In his preface he adroitly substitutes 'kaitito whiti'(singer)
for 'taniwha' in the venerable proverb 'Waikato taniwha rau, he piko he
taniwha', so that there is not a monster but a poet at every bend of the

river. What's more, he has embraced Ngāti Kaitito Whiti as his tribe and organised a really satisfying hui where the rangatira (Vincent O'Sullivan, Bob Orr, Murray Edmond) make strong statements, as expected, but younger and/or less assured voices are also given the chance to speak and often surprise and impress with their power. Moods range from anger, grief and bittersweet reminiscence to the cheeky hilarity of John Leyland's 'Light Relief', in which the business card of a prominent Hamilton mortgage-broker (a real person, easily found on Google) is spied floating in a urinal.

The country's fiercest fighting during the colonial era took place in the Waikato region. The blood-drenched history of land confiscations is a dark knowledge that the contributors share. Former Ruakura scientist Barry Smith refers in a footnote to his poem 'This Good Friday' to a particularly shameful incident: the pitiless bayoneting of wounded Ōrākau defenders by imperial troops. I think you can hear their ghosts keening in the background throughout the whole anthology.

The injustices of the nineteenth century have continuing effects and still rankle, but the ire is tempered throughout the book by a compassionate understanding of how individual lives are shaped by political forces beyond their control. Piet Nieuwland's 'The Confiscation Line' is a good example, aware of the theft while humanely considering the descendants of Private John Arnold (another real person, worth looking up in the Cambridge Museum's website).

Several contributors look from the colonial past to the still-colonising present. Elaine Riddell warns in 'Morning Glory' that this introduced convolvulus, however heart-shaped and pretty, prevents the growth of 'tōtara, rimu, karaka'. Celia Hope dreams in 'Succession' of a time when native flax and 'mighty kahikatea' will reclaim contested space from English poplars. My eye keeps coming back to the book's clever cover image by Patricia Canlas Wu (Rapatahana's Hong Kong-based daughter), which shows a Holstein-Friesian cow standing right in the Waikato River and turning its head to gaze at the reader. It serves simultaneously as a reminder that the region's beef and dairy industry developed largely from confiscated land,

and a symbol of today's concerns about methane emission levels and polluted waterways.

The world, of course, keeps changing. You focus hard on one region and gradually the whole globe comes into view. The once-domineering 'Pax Britannica' mentioned by Nieuwland has dwindled into confused little England botching Brexit. Meanwhile power struggles elsewhere have led to fresh migrations, altering the ethnic mix of the planet, including the Waikato. There's a lovely moment in Hamilton poet Richard Selnikoff's 'Fairfield Shops' (written three years before the Christchurch mosque shootings) when a young Māori woman in a heavy metal T-shirt is spied 'eating ice cream and laughing together' with her hijab-wearing Middle Eastern friend.

Wine reviewer Michael Cooper has long included a 'best buys' category in his buyer's guide. Should *Poetry New Zealand* decide to introduce an equivalent, *Ngā Kupu Waikato* has to be one of the top contenders of recent years. At $15 it's outrageous value. You need a copy.

Elizabeth Morton

# Eleanor Rimoldi

Eleanor Rimoldi
*American Retrospective: Poems 1961–2016*
Hicksville Press, 2018
RRP $25, 55pp

Eleanor Rimoldi's writing is peripatetic itch and biographic wandering. This is a poet on the periphery of things — who is neither here nor there. It is a collection of movement, of transitional spaces. She chronicles her move from the United States to New Zealand, shifts in her relationship status, the arrival of children, and the changing schedules of daily life. Such content could be viewed as quaint in its autobiographical specificity. One might suggest its distribution be constrained to a few family and friends. Such counsel would, however, belie the quiet magic of the poems here, and the convincing narrative of the life at their heart.

Rimoldi's poetry is comfort food. It is gentle and familiar and doesn't repeat on its reader. It has a sentimentality and a sense of the shape of history — in its macrocosmic and microcosmic forms. Family is central; there is a poem for her daughter, 'Homework', which is a sort of philoprogenitive celebration of 'the bone, the flesh of my making', the 'independent mind'. There is a poem about the poetry of celestial observation, for her son, Alex, and an adulatory poem to her other child, Dylan, wherein goldfish meet with fact and fiction. There is even a cat. These poems invite their reader into their living room, and into their lives, with a soft intimacy and an endearing humility. It's seldom I make such a judgment on the basis of poetic output, but I reckon I like Eleanor Rimoldi a lot.

Certainly, there are moments when the narrative seems a little too temporally neat. I feel like giving the poems a shake, shooing away the need for citation and explication. I want to allow a lengthier leash, give them a day-pass to wherever they wish to wander. This is not to suggest the poems are in themselves deficient. They are, actually, quite wonderful, and my reading was sustained by their honesty and verbal dexterity. It is, rather, an over-abundance of context that muddies the proverbial waters.

The first poem in the collection, 'American Retrospective', is profoundly inventive. It has some gorgeous images, with sensual adjectives buddied up with unlikely nouns — 'curdled pity', 'knotted fumbling', 'unshaved morning', 'fading limbos', 'hollowed echoes'. Rimoldi's language here is at its most visceral:

no tears shed
save those
that fall unsalted
in musty rusted cist

There are adventures into the political, with references to the racism of the United States — in particular the racial segregation, police discrimination, and the subsequent civil unrest that manifested as the Watts Riots of 1965. In 'There is a Precedent', 'Black homesteaders rise / out of white graves / to beat out a clearing / in the forest of our deceit'. In 'Meditations in the Maternity Ward', Rimoldi speaks of herself as a 'white liberal' who is 'fevered with inaction'. She gives a nod to T. S. Eliot's *The Hollow Men* with her 'Between the conception and the creation / Falls the shadow'. There is a sense of a writer bearing witness to the passage of history, 'passive and mute'. The gestation, in this poem, is both literal and figurative. The coming child is also the emergence of a new beginning for a more empathetic, active and societally engaged generation — or such is the hope.

Where the poetry moves away from the large-scale sociological, anthropological or political, it is fleecy and soft, though, sometimes, with a gloriously affecting final turn. 'Something Happened to a Child' is one such poem. The description in this is rich, with sections that prickle the senses:

Many miles, years away I remembered still the big house
the wood burning stove, cinnamon
smell of straw and dung in the milking shed
horse's breath and leather, sun baked skin perfume.

This poem concludes with a revisit of the 'big house', and the finding is vague and tragic. The title returns to haunt the piece.

A couple of poems in this collection are hampered by their simplicity. The cat poem, for instance, is a beautiful description of a cat's predations, but goes no further. A poem such as 'Involuntary Committal', by contrast, has an additional tier of emotion, and sets the reader an ambush at its conclusion. It is sentimentally loaded, and splits the reader's sympathies two ways, creating a compelling tug-o-war.

Rimoldi is a temperate poet. Her work does not shout into a loudspeaker directed from the rooftops. Rather, her work speaks quietly, and so we lean in close. *American Retrospective* has us leaning in for 55 years, across continents, and in various familial guises. It has warmth, observational prowess, intelligence, and a whole lot of love. It is a journey on which I'm extremely glad to have been invited.

## Tracey Slaughter / Lynn Davidson

Tracey Slaughter
*Conventional Weapons*
Victoria University Press, 2019
RRP $25, 95pp

Lynn Davidson
*Islander*
Victoria University Press, 2019
RRP $25, 80pp

*Conventional Weapons* is technically Tracey Slaughter's first full poetry collection. However, she is no novice — she has been publishing poetry for over two decades and works as a lecturer in creative writing at Waikato University. Tracey was the featured poet in *Poetry New Zealand 25* (2002) and her first book, *Her body rises* (2005), included both stories and poems. She has received multiple awards, including the international Bridport Prize in 2014, a 2007 New Zealand Book Month Award, and Katherine Mansfield Awards in 2004 and 2001.

Slaughter's poetry is dark, lyrical, sexy, and urban gothic with desperation and raw pain. In an inexperienced poet's hands this might be expressed in a less controlled way, but she keeps a tight rein on her poems — these aren't uncrafted outbursts on the page. The poems express complex characters and dramatic monologues from a range of women who are frequently pushed to their limits.

In an interview, Slaughter has described the collection as being 'constructed around different stories. It has a backbone of three long cycles of poems, of different people who have had different traumatic experiences.' The poems often feel violent and leave the reader feeling uncomfortable. Eating disorders, abortion, trauma, widowhood, sex in cheap hotels — it feels as if Slaughter is bearing witness for vulnerable young women. She sits in their skin, feels their hunger, embodies and laments their pain, often with unpredictable language and imagery, which brings the reader back to revisit, unpick and unfold.

A poem like 'nursery' clashes nursery rhymes and the naïveté of childhood with lost innocence so skillfully and with such a joy in language's musicality and rhythm that there is beauty in the awful brokenness. It is perhaps no surprise that Slaughter is a musician, a drummer like one of her characters, Karen Carpenter. Her long sequence 'it was the seventies when me & Karen Carpenter hung out' makes up almost a quarter of the book: 'me & Karen Carpenter / . . . We loaded our skin / & rubbed in the limits like cream, microscoped / for layouts of handbag & muscle. We could / not switch off the mirrors'. In this long sequence, the narrator and Karen Carpenter negotiate youth, eating disorders and a messed-up home life together, 'Handholds / of knucklebone settled / into our throats', until finally 'We metabolise our / hearts.'

Hearts are a reoccurring motif in the collection, from Karen Carpenter's heart attack to the abortion of '31 reasons not to hear a heartbeat' to the broken heart of 'the mine wife' to the heart that won't go on in 'a woman walks into a bar'. Some women find a way to survive and some don't. 'the mine wife', another long poem, features the wife of a miner lost in the Pike River disaster. Here we don't get a conventional broken heart; we get to see the full complexity of a relationship — good and bad — in the grieving. The wife remembers snapping 'what's [love] when it's at / home then' to her husband when he proposed. No rose-tinted glasses here.

The young women in this collection fight for some kind of agency in their lives, like Ophelia in 'conventional weapons' who 'will make you fucking                    sorry'. What are a young woman's conventional weapons? Their sexuality? Their bravery? Their attitude? Their resilience? All of these things? Slaughter manages to capture both the vulnerability and the razor-sharp toughness of young women, allowing these attributes to sit side-by-side rather than cancel one or the other out.

Like the cover image by Paul Alsop of the young girl with a superhero mask painted on and a stubborn set to her mouth, these young women are tough, they are their own heroes, and nobody is rescuing them but themselves.

Reading Tracey Slaughter's book alongside that of Lynn Davidson, I initially thought they were so different there would be little intersection. However, on a second reading I began to notice the way both poets use repetition to great effect. For example, Tracey Slaughter writes:

> Call your wife, leave a message at the sob. Call your wife, she is learning the hard way. Call your wife, the histology is back. Call your wife, her lipstick is audible. Call your wife, she's on her third bottle & the kids are starting to look like stars.

In the opening poem, 'she is currently living' 'in a dead-end off jellicoe. in the waiting room of blue vinyl fear. she is currently living in supermarket flowers that whisper buy me in their middle-class plastic. she is currently living in a red metal playpen riding her stepsister's rocking horse'. And: 'a woman walks into a bar & the red ball slips into the corner pocket. a woman walks into a bar twice bitten & wipes the vinyl stool with her wrist. a woman walks into a bar & shaves her head on the dance floor'. These poems drive the reader onwards, and each repetition creates new meaning and possibilities. There is a sense of urgency that increases with each chanted phrase.

Lynn Davidson also employs a very deliberate use of repetition in her work. In fact, the use of repetition in poetry was a focus of her PhD thesis. Lynn's new collection *Islander* is a meditation on home, nesting and migration. There is not one home in *Islander*; the collection travels between Scotland, Australia and New Zealand. Land, sea and cultures are bridged in the poems. The collection is structured in five sections. From *Light* and *Bonefire*, it then transitions to earth in *Return to Islay*, roots itself in *Standing Places*, then deeper in *Bass Rock*, where the final poem returns in the final line to the children:

My loves
My light
My dearest islanders

I know I'm not the only reviewer to notice the similarities between
Lynn and Dinah Hawken: both are closely attuned to the natural world
and time. Lynn's poem 'The word' explicitly responds to Dinah 'we call
light / light. // And especially when it goes out': often in Lynn's work,
language and meaning — our understanding of, and fragile place in, the
natural world — feel vitally connected. The poem 'Ancient light' makes
me think of the time starlight takes to reach Earth, then in 'Pearls'

Time goes slower in the sea
and faster in the mountains.
Physics has taken over
where poetry left off.

Lynn's poems are quiet, reserved and measured, and her landscapes
are populated with family — a father falling ill, a lover, children leaving
home. Again, language makes the world real. In 'Leaving Wellington':

Hours go by and elements still gather.
Each day my waking children, just by naming
assembled all the solid things of world:
the bath, stove, chair, the bed, the window,
the shoe, the dinosaur, the door, the wall.
Then in a kind of via negative
they composed two empty rooms by leaving home.

I said it was an anchor but it's not.
It's a shadow roughly like a kiss.

In 'New Feats of Horsemanship', the lines 'later I learned about echoes /
and etymology.' reinforce the connections between repetition, language

and concrete meaning more explicitly. Then, in 'Even though it's not the beginning of the world anymore', the 'Ancient light' returns 'lapping in from space' and the skewed repetition:

> An opening in the wall for the admission of light
> An opening in the wall or the admission of light
> An opening in the wall for the obstruction of fear

Each repetition is a new iteration, it's a shift in meaning and creates a new moment in the poem. Each repetition opens up possibilities for people and places. This, coupled with the sense of movement between places and people and time, allows meaning to be constantly shifting, allowing for multiplicity of identity, and perhaps allows us to hold onto those we have lost. Repetition can cast a spell or call out a prayer.

Birds make constant appearances throughout the collection. They fly and come home to roost, to nest — 'Those birds soaring, looking for a space to land'. In 'A hillside of houses leave', birds and homes morph into one:

> Steeped in old weather the wooden houses
> remember their bird-selves and unfold
> barely-jointed wings.

Inside the bird-home lie people curled 'inside / the bones that keep them / that will not keep them long'. There is an aching impermanence. Children are 'thin air away / . . . and then they flew / and shone'.

Again, in 'Return' 'all the white-washed houses / are birds / standing on one leg'. Birds are children, birds search for home, birds are home. Birds sighted from a ship at sea mean that land is near.

I think this is Lynn Davidson's best collection of poetry to date. There is fragility but a steely core; wild nature but humanely populated. Time and place and meaning keep shifting, and the poet somehow makes her way through this loss and change, finding meaning in the journey, finding home where her heart roosts.

## Rachel Tobin

Rachel Tobin
*Say It Naked*
Submarine Poetry, Mākaro Press, 2018
RRP $25, 79pp

If there is a soul, *Say It Naked* might be its biopsy and tonic. The poetry here is an uncovering, but also a piecing together — and Rachel Tobin knows that in order to suture a wound, one needs to first glean its location. The tetraptych — four parts of sensuality and breath and beating heart — bears the sensitivity and concinnous weighting of an artist. Indeed, Tobin's own figure-work bookends each section. Bodies, naked and vulnerable, stalk the pages like signposts to the poetry's raw centre. *Look*, they seem to say. *Look*. The figure-work, while elegant and true to the poetry, is not requisite. These poems know how to speak for themselves.

This is remarkable, because these poems were from a period of time during which Tobin lost her physical voice. Yet there is nothing taciturn here. Tobin talks with a clear candour about the milestones and markers of a life.

Tobin's poetic world oscillates between binaries. It is generous and pithy; it is imaginative and honest; it is a wayfaring and the home turf. There is a core strength to its vulnerability. The world is embodied; the human subject is an artefact of the natural world. Tobin's poetry is at its fiercest where the poems are not pointedly about season or nature; and yet where they are precisely that — but through the lens of grief, love and human error.

Her poem 'Ashes', which won the New Zealand Poetry Society International Competition in 2012, is one such instance of this adroit filtration, with a profound sense of whenua, as it is touched by familial loss. This is a sestina — a form notoriously tricky but, in this instance, ostensibly effortless. It has not lost oomph to form. It has an ancestral pull, an earthiness that holds the generations: 'where your father's and your father's father's passing / are marked by stone and wild grasses of a salt-stained room'.

There is a witchery of nouns, in this poem and in others — exotic and familiar. There are coal hods and fire koans and windicators and Iroquoian lullabies. The words, stitched together, have a buttery quality. They are luxuriant on the tongue, and I want to frame each one and set it on my mantelpiece. On occasion Tobin breaks her lines hard and fast, but the music is not cast adrift. The line breaks bring some kind of respite from the fullness.

In 'Our father', the lines are pruned in such a way that the poem is spindly, and the meaning stamped out in a more marked manner. Every break is considered and each line gifts some kind of image. The poem is 'after Grahame Sydney', and this shows in its pictorial intensity:

His old crib
digs its elbows
into the hill's breast


The personification here is not mere poetic plaything. Rather, it speaks to the worldview at the heart of the collection — a sort of conceptualisation of the boundaries between human and Earth as nebulous. A sense of *tat tvam asi* or 'thou art that' pervades the work. The person is embedded in their environment and vice versa. This grounding makes the expressly ecological works all the harder-hitting. 'On behalf of . . .' is one such poem, and concerns climate change, mining, fracking and acidification:

I heard today the shells of molluscs
making a living there are dissolving

I heard today trees are learning
to take up more carbon dioxide

The content here is expansive, but is no less proximate in feeling. That said, the cluster of poems that comprise the third section, *behind the pose*, are sometimes lacking the raw grunt and grit of the other sections. In their quest to strip away pretence and arrive at some truth, they feel more premeditated, more affected.

Poems like 'What's left' show the poet at her most potent. This is an inventory of absence, but there is something resolute here. This is about death, about the dissonance that comes with difficult relationships, but also about the way small things butt in on dying, and the way the world soldiers on irrespective. The poem sets about establishing an ambiguous bond, a drug regimen, a decay and a sketch of the man at its heart. It leaves us with this:

> A cat flap gapes in a forgotten cottage.
> A door squeaks.
> A letterbox stands strong against a city wind.
> A thousand windows open, just right.
> A woman with five children
> grows strong in self-forgetting.

Rachel Tobin's first collection is wise and strong and full-frontal stark-naked. It is beautifully balanced, and it knows the best way to a reader's heart is not by any circuitous route. The book itself is an exquisite artefact with an artistry that makes for a stunning aesthetic. Tobin may have lost her voice, but she never lost her ability for verbal clout and sensitivity.

Elisabeth Kumar

## Kirsten Warner

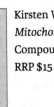

Kirsten Warner
*Mitochondrial Eve*
Compound Press, 2018
RRP $15

In this spacious collection, Kirsten Warner gazes into the depths of an overwhelming past and negotiates a kind of tension between survival and hope. Pulled on the one side toward some thorny void, prehistory with its lack of judgement, and the relief of death, and caught on the other side in the rich tangle of animal life, these poems are drawn out wide so we can follow each thread.

Compound Press's production is beautiful, although a bit embarrassed by a garbled block of back copy that refers inexplicably to 'these impacted poems'. Between the covers, the language is spare and careful. There is a feeling of relentless realism, feet in West Auckland mud, stories that take up time because they just do. The six poems aren't necessarily related, but they speak with one distinctive voice, and beg to be spoken aloud — more than one evokes childhood skipping rhymes, and all have an easy rhythm. Warner soaks up experiences and identities in gorgeously observational detail, but, although her poems are crafted skilfully, she stops before they could become over-processed.

> I step over cracks so I won't marry a Jack
> resist walking out into traffic
> we don't have a bath and I'd have to find blades
> and it's an end I want not intensification
> someone to find me before I drift away.

That's arguably not the heaviest topic dropped into these poems, but it is typical of Warner's light touch — she trusts herself and her readers, and doesn't ask for help, just for witness. She dreams of driving a bulldozer, 'spreading the weight evenly / so I never get stuck' in the clay of the mucky past; up her sleeve, a strong Westie teleology: 'Spread good dark soil, pick up dry leaves, hold a baby'.

Perhaps this is why this collection doesn't feel indulgent — she doesn't lose touch with the voices of hope, 'women who make music . . . / common acts of decency / keeping an eye on history', her own daughter's reassurance in the face of what hints at gut-dropping trauma: 'so don't worry / it all turns out okay'. Nor does she fall into platitude or easy answers, if there are answers at all. The most abrupt moment in the collection is at the end of 'S.O.S.', after a grim depiction of climate change ('my shoes may not last / nor life as we know it's // one straight line / to gulf stream warming'); in the absence of anything 'the last / woman' can do about it, Warner gives her final direction, and stops there. 'Don't blink.'

Elsewhere, though, it's humanity in action. In 'Off the Leash', she strides into a story and then veers away to a remembered and tender portrait of a dog being muzzled. Warner sees in that moment a familiar curse, or a cursed familiar: pain placed on another from outside and worn on the body as a foreign thing, with the sufferer's response dictated (the dog forcibly 'puzzled' in a rhyming act of coercion).

> the pet shop assistant patting,
> tender with the pink plastic cage
> down on his knees
> slipping one finger under the edge
> saying a dog doesn't really mind,
> grooming her for it
> on and off
> soft mouth and nose
> the dog's puzzled brown eyes
> staring straight ahead.

Warner has no time for this kind of gormless benevolence. She responds with her whole being, takes her own liberty, cradles the power of the experience — a trucking yard flirtation — along with the weight of 'marriage, / and all the years of love' that pull her away from it. It's enough to be unleashed.

If Warner's narrator 'surface[d] dismantled' in the first poem, she ends the collection reconstructed in community — in a feral lineage from the eponymous Eve through Katherine Mansfield and Mata Hari and back to Nut (the sky-goddess, not the broken eccentric who might first come to mind — although I sense Warner is proud to be both).

## Pat White

Pat White
*Watching for the Wingbeat: New and selected poems*
Cold Hub Press, 2018
RRP $39.95, 162pp

Pat White's new book of selected poems covers 40 years of his writing life, from *Signposts* in 1977 to *Fracking & Hawk* in 2015, together with some uncollected and unpublished work.

The first impression it gives is continuity. White's preoccupations have, it seems, always been what they are now: landscape, love, history, the natural world.

A great deal of care has clearly gone into winnowing out the best pieces from this lifetime of work. It would be very hard to find a false note. It is nevertheless true that there's an austerity about the earliest poems here which has been modulated and complicated by White's experiments with the long line in more recent times. Take, for instance, an early poem such as 'Paperbacks':

That was the summer
when the paperbacks grew mould
from the damp
of the outhouse floor

. . .

when graduation took its leave
of student flats
with cheap editions
of expensive ideals . . .

This is a wonderful piece: spare, telling, making the single image of these 'grubby books / that fed our empty heads' stand for a whole world of adult responsibilities, leavened by a spine of humorous self-deprecation.

And yet, when you contrast it with a more recent poem such as 'Getting out of the car, Danseys Pass', you can see how much these years of practice, of constant circling in on that central mystery of concise expression, have done for the strength and flexibility of his idiom:

> A shingle road winding through mist on hills
> tussock beside the cutting, silhouette against
> a drop down to Maerewhenua Stream
> cutting deeper than epiphany
> through schist
> and the other side of the road
> in drizzling rain

This evocation of the joys — and complexities — of 'following this road / in search of God knows what' is on a different order of suggestiveness and complexity than the early poems, fine though they are.

There's nothing 'simple' about the experiences presented here, and nothing casual about the musical skill with which the words are modulated, almost like one of Beethoven's late quartets.

But what is Pat White *about* as a poet? Pastoral, once a byword for escapism and irrelevance, has become one of the central modes of our time: whether in the guise of dystopian 'eco-poetry' or utopian nostalgia. Is that why White seems suddenly so relevant? So armoured by integrity against the accusations of complacency and self-regard that can afflict other poets attempting so comprehensive a summing-up of their achievement?

I would argue that pastoral concerns have only ever been part of his worldview. In a poem such as 'For my children', for instance, he scores a rather dismal and unsought rhyme with some *very* topical concerns:

One year when things were tight
that old rifle was sold. It was no
accident, but contemplation of
cut throats, fascination
with destruction has marked
itself into the marrow
of too many generations.

Gun enthusiasts can't understand why the rest of us show so little sympathy when they moan about the compulsory loss of their pretties. My father was a gun-nut, so I think I know a few things about the type. To *him*, an old rifle or musket was a miracle of applied engineering, a beautiful piece of craftmanship with only the most tenuous relationship to its original function. To *me*, it was an instrument of death which I could hardly bear to put my hands on. It reeked of blood.

White's poem concludes:

If you visited me now, there
is a garden to sit in, a drink
to share, and talking to do.
Across the bay, a bluff
where rock crumbles, is
shaping trees' stubborn growth.

There's no heirloom to argue over.
There had to be a time to halt
the darkness of such bitter games.

By no stretch of the imagination could this be described as a propaganda poem, but it *is*, I suppose, polemical in these times of compulsory buy-backs of firearms in the wake of the March 2019 Christchurch terror attack. But it makes its point so gently that it would be hard to reject the idyllic vision of those last few lines.

The point is that White *knows*. He knows why people love their guns. *I* don't love them, but I did love my father, and I respect the sincerity of his attachment to the aesthetics of these ambassadors from a not-too-distant past. Those 'bitter games' at the end of the poem ring very true, also.

It's a commonplace that Scottish families always fall out over wills and heirlooms (not that I suppose it's a purely Scottish trait). I had an aunt who went mad when she wasn't left the pieces of furniture she wanted in another of my ancestors' wills. Guns, bad blood — it's all in the poem. That's one of the many reasons why I love Pat White's work, and find it a continuing source of inspiration. It feels very close to me.

I'll conclude with some lines from another one of his great this-is-the-state-of-things-for-me-now poems, 'Elemental'. Midway through, he evokes 'a poet who wrote / hawk-like, no longer in need / of predatory advice, able to spiral / onto a stray word, sneak it from the set'. The words could apply just as easily to White himself.

Like *that* poet (T. S. Eliot, Seamus Heaney, Ted Hughes? — certain internal references to *Four Quartets* would suggest the first), he's very definitely 'not shovelling bullshit':

> It's difficult to forget how much we know
> and look at the site as if for the first time
> to catch the flow but not the flood
>          nobody told me
> it never got easier, this putting on the page.

If you are intending to read Pat White, this is the book to buy. If you're not, I have to say that you're missing a treat: a collection that brings together poems that are beautiful, unassuming and perfectly paced, all at the same time.

# About the Contributors

**Johanna Aitchison** has been writing for half her life. She was recently awarded a Mark Strand Scholarship in poetry. Johanna is currently working on a PhD in Creative Writing at Massey University, with the topic 'Disrupting Voices, Making Meaning: Erasures, Anagrams, and Alter Egos in Contemporary Postmodern Poetry'. Her poems have previously been published in *Sport, Landfall, Turbine | Kapohau* and *Best New Zealand Poems*, and she has a short story in the US-based anthology *Best Small Fictions 2019*.

**Rosetta Allan** completed a Master's in Creative Writing at the University of Auckland with First Class Honours in 2017, and was awarded a Sir James Wallace Master of Creative Writing Scholarship. Her bestseller debut novel, *Purgatory*, was published in 2014. Rosetta was recently the first New Zealand writer in residence at the St Petersburg Art Residency in Russia. Her second novel, *The Unreliable People*, was released in May 2019 by Penguin Books and has become a bestseller. In 2019, she was the Creative NZ/University of Waikato Writer in Residence.

**John Allison** was born in Blenheim in 1950. He returned from Melbourne in mid-2016 after 15 years. Prior to that, he'd had poems published in more than 200 literary journals in New Zealand and overseas. He was the featured poet in *Poetry NZ 14*. He has had five collections of poetry published: *Dividing the Light: Poems 1986–93* (Hazard Press, 1997); *Both Roads Taken* (Sudden Valley Press, 1997); *Stone Moon Dark Water* (Sudden Valley Press, 1999); *Balance* (Five Islands Press, 2006); and *A Place to Return To* (Cold Hub Press, 2019). A collection of essays on perception, imagination and poetry, *A Way of Seeing*, was published by Lindisfarne Press, Great Barrington, MA, in 2003.

**Ivy Alvarez** is the author of *The Everyday English Dictionary* (Paekakariki Press, 2016), *Hollywood Starlet* (dancing girl press, 2015), *Disturbance* (Seren, 2013) and *Mortal* (Red Morning Press, 2006). Her latest, *Diaspora: Volume L*, is available from Paloma Press (California, 2019). www.ivyalvarez.com.

**Hamish Ansley** is a sometimes-poet and writer of short fiction. He completed a Master's thesis about masculinity in contemporary fiction at the University of Waikato in 2017. He was long-listed for the 2019 National Flash Fiction Day prize, placed third in the first annual Sargeson prize, and has words in *Poetry New Zealand, Mayhem, Sweet Mammalian, Flash Frontier* and *Foodcourt.*

**Ruth Arnison** is the afternoon administrator at Knox College in Dunedin. She is the editor of *Poems in the Waiting Room* (NZ) and the founder of Lilliput Libraries.

**Stu Bagby** is a former winner of the New Zealand Poetry Society's International Competition. First published nationally in *AUP New Poets 2*, he has written four books of poetry and a play, and has edited three anthologies. He lives in Paremoremo.

**Cindy Botha** lives in Tauranga. She started writing very late in life, and has found the companionship of a sharp pencil and a lined notepad to be an incomparable delight.

**Liz Breslin** writes plays, poems, stories and a fortnightly column, 'Thinking Allowed', for *The Otago Daily Times.* Her poetry collection, *Alzheimer's and a spoon* (Otago University Press, 2017), was listed as one of the *New Zealand Listener's* Top 100 Books of 2017. Liz's recent performances include *Love in a time of netball* and a stint as the back end of Jill the Cow for her 2018 pantomime, *Jac and the Beansprouts.* www.lizbreslin.com.

**Iain Britton** is the author of five collections of poetry. His poems have been published or are forthcoming in *Landfall, brief, New Zealand Review of Books, Harvard Review, Poetry* (Chicago), *Jacket2, The New York Times, Stand, Agenda, Poetry Wales* and John Tranter's *Journal of Poetics Research* (Australia). *The Intaglio Poems* was published by Hesterglock Press (UK) in 2017.

**Owen Bullock** has published three collections of poetry, five books of haiku and a novella; the most recent being *Summer Haiku* (2019) and *Work & Play* (2017). He currently teaches creative writing at the University of Canberra. He has a website for his research into poetry and process: www.poetry-in-process.com/

**Marisa Cappetta** graduated suma cum laude from the Hagley Writers' Institute and received a mentorship from the New Zealand Society of Authors. She has published poems in journals and anthologies in New Zealand and internationally. Her first collection, *How to tour the world on a flying fox*, was published by Steele Roberts Aotearoa in 2016. She has completed a second collection, *Windows below the waterline.*

**Peter Clague** is an Aucklander by birth, an educator by calling, and a poet by necessity. As antidote to city life, for 50 years he has been a disciple of mountains, pilgrim to rivers. When no one is watching, he worships trees. Although his mind and body are currently residing overseas for a spell, his heart still dwells in a shaded bivy, halfway down a tawa-speckled ridge, above the whispering forks of an unseen stream.

**Britt Scott Clark** is an actress and writer from Auckland. She has been performing since the age of 18, and has appeared in a number of productions both in New Zealand and abroad. In her time off, she is pursuing, passionately, a creative writing degree at Massey University.

**Aidan Coleman** is a member of the J. M. Coetzee Centre for Creative Practice at the University of Adelaide. His third book of poems, *Mount Sumptuous*, has recently been published by Wakefield Press, and he is currently writing a biography of the poet John Forbes.

**Jennifer Compton** was born in Wellington and now lives in Melbourne. She is a poet and playwright who also writes prose.

**Jeni Curtis** is a Christchurch writer whose work has been published in various publications including *takahē*, New Zealand Poetry Society anthologies, *JAAM*, *Atlanta Review*, *The London Grip*, *Shot Glass Journal* and *Poetry New Zealand Yearbook*. She is a graduate of the Hagley Writers' Institute, Christchurch. In 2016 she received a mentorship from the New Zealand Society of Authors to put together a collection of poems. She is secretary of the Canterbury Poets Collective, chair of the *takahē* trust and co-editor of poetry for *takahē*.

**Semira Davis** is a queer writer. Her poetry has appeared in *Re-Draft*, *Ika*, *Landfall*, *Blackmail Press*, *takahē*, *Poetry New Zealand Yearbook*, and *The Friday Poem*. She was a New Zealand Society of Authors mentorship recipient for 2019.

**Lynn Davidson** is a New Zealand writer living in Edinburgh. She writes poetry, fiction and essays. Her most recent collection of poetry, *Islander*, was published by Shearsman Books in the United Kingdom and Victoria University Press in New Zealand. Lynn had a Hawthorden Fellowship in 2013 and a Bothy Project Residency in 2016. Lynn teaches creative writing, works in Edinburgh libraries, and is a member of 12, a feminist poetry collective.

**Alison Denham** lives in Dunedin, a city she loves more and more as time goes on. Her work has appeared in poetry journals and anthologies in New Zealand, the United Kingdom and the United States. In 2014 her second collection of poems, *Raspberry Money*, was published by Sudden Valley Press, Canterbury Poets Collective.

**Allan Drew** teaches creative writing and academic writing at Massey University. He completed his PhD in English at Victoria University of Wellington in 2017; his thesis focused on methods of characterisation in early modern narrative poetry. Allan lives in Auckland with his wife and daughter. You can read some of his fiction, poems and non-fiction via his website, www.allan-drew.com.

**Doc Drumheller** was born in Charleston, South Carolina, and has lived in New Zealand for more than half his life. He has worked in award-winning groups for theatre and music, and has published 10 collections of poetry. His poems have been translated into more than 20 languages, and he has performed in Cuba, Lithuania, Italy, Hungary, Bulgaria, Romania, Japan, India, China, Nicaragua, the United States, Mexico, El Salvador, and widely throughout New Zealand. He lives in Oxford, Canterbury, where he edits and publishes the literary journal *Catalyst.*

**David Eggleton** is a Dunedin-based writer, critic and poet. His most recent collection of poetry is *Edgeland and Other Poems*, with artwork by James Robinson, published by Otago University Press in 2018. He is the Poet Laureate 2019–2021.

**Johanna Emeney** works at Massey University as a teacher of creative writing. She also co-facilitates the Michael King Young Writers Programme with Rosalind Ali. Her background is in English literature teaching, and her main research interest is in the medical humanities as it relates to poetry. Her two books of poetry are *Apple & Tree* (Cape Catley, 2011) and *Family History* (Mākaro Press, 2017).

**Ben Evans** played American football for Colgate University before earning an MFA from the University of Oregon. His poems have appeared (or soon will) in *Colorado Review, The Cortland Review, Fourteen Hills, Sugar House Review, RHINO, Ekphrasis* and elsewhere. A nascent librettist and longtime editor of the arts review *Fogged Clarity*, he lived and wrote in the South Island of New Zealand for three months in 2017. Currently he lives in Muskegon, Michigan, with his hound, Jack.

**Annabelle Fenn** is a Year 13 student at Woodford House, Havelock North.

**Rachel J. Fenton** lives in Auckland. Her poetry has been shortlisted for the Royal Society of New Zealand Manhire Prize, the Fish Poetry Prize judged by Paul Durcan, runner-up in the Ambit Summer Competition judged by

Sarah Howe, long-listed for *The Rialto* Nature Poetry Competition judged by Michael Longley, and published in *Landfall, English, Journal of the English Association* (Oxford Academic), *The Rialto,* and *Magma.*

**Meagan France** is an Auckland-based writer of European and Māori descent born and raised in Perth, Western Australia. She moved permanently to New Zealand in 2005, where she has lived with her partner and two children since. Meagan's fiction and poetry have been published in *Landfall, Geometry, Phantom Billstickers Café Reader* and *takahē.* Meagan has a Master's in Creative Writing from the University of Auckland, and was a recipient of a 2019 emerging writers residency at the Michael King Writers Centre. She is currently working on her first novel.

**Rebecca Ruth Gould** is the author of the poetry collection *Cityscapes* (Alien Buddha Press, 2019) and the award-winning monograph *Writers & Rebels* (Yale University Press, 2016). She has translated many books from Persian and Georgian, including *After Tomorrow the Days Disappear: Ghazals and Other Poems of Hasan Sijzi of Delhi* (Northwestern University Press, 2016) and *The Death of Bagrat Zakharych and other Stories* by Vazha-Pshavela (Paper & Ink, 2019). A Pushcart Prize nominee, she was a finalist for the Luminaire Award for Best Poetry (2017) and for Lunch Ticket's Gabo Prize (2017).

**Michael Hall** lives in Dunedin. Recent poems have appeared in *Landfall, The Otago Daily Times* and *The Friday Poem: 100 New Zealand Poems,* edited by Steve Braunias.

**Jordan Hamel** is a Pōneke-based poet and performer. He was raised in Timaru on a diet of Catholicism and masculine emotional repression. He is the current New Zealand Poetry Slam champion, a poetry editor for *Barren Magazine* and has words published in *Sport, takahē, Mayhem, Sweet Mammalian, Mimicry, Glass Poetry, Queen Mob's Teahouse* and elsewhere.

**Michael Hanne** founded the Comparative Literature Programme at the University of Auckland in 1995. He currently teaches the medical humanities course 'Unexamined Metaphors, Uncharted Stories' with Elisabeth Kumar at the Faculty of Medical and Health Sciences. His recent research has focused on the role of narrative and metaphor in the construction of a wide range of disciplines from medicine to politics, to education and the law. See his latest project at narrativemetaphornexus. weebly.com.

**Emma Harris** lives in Dunedin with her husband and children. She teaches English and is an assistant principal at Columba College. Her poetry has previously been published in *Southern Ocean Review, Blackmail Press* and *Poetry New Zealand*.

**Matthew Harris** lives in Dunedin, teaches online academic and creative writing for Massey University, and writes short fictions.

**Paula Harris** lives in Palmerston North, where she writes poems and sleeps in a lot, because that's what depression makes you do. She won the 2018 Janet B. McCabe Poetry Prize and the 2017 Lilian Ida Smith Award. Her writing has been published in various journals, including *Berfrois, Queen Mob's Teahouse, The Rialto, Barren, Kissing Dynamite, SWWIM, Glass, Aotearotica, The Spinoff* and *Landfall*. See more of her work at: www.paulaharris.co.nz; @paulaoffkilter (Twitter); @ paulaharris_poet (Instagram); and @paulaharrispoet (Facebook).

**Poppy Hayward** is a Year 12 student at Logan Park High School, Dunedin.

**Helen Heath**'s debut collection of poetry, *Graft*, was published in 2012 by Victoria University Press to critical acclaim. *Graft* won the NZSA Jessie Mackay Best First Book for Poetry award in 2013, and was the first book of fiction or poetry to be shortlisted for the Royal Society of New Zealand Science Book Prize, also in 2013. Helen's poetry and essays have been published in many journals in New Zealand, Australia, the

United Kingdom and the United States. Her latest book, *Are Friends Electric?*, won the 2019 Peter and Mary Biggs Poetry Award at the 2019 Ockham New Zealand Book Awards.

**Chris Holdaway** is a poet and bookmaker from Northland. He is the author of *HIGH-TENSION/FASHION* (Greying Ghost, 2018) and directs Compound Press in Auckland.

**Chelsea Houghton** lives in Rangiora, North Canterbury, with her husband and children. She is currently a Master's student in Creative Writing at Massey University. Her fiction and poetry have appeared in *Cordite, Mimicry, Oscen, Flash Frontier* and *X-R-A-Y Literary Magazine*.

**John Howell** lives in Ngaio, Wellington. His first book of published poems was *Homeless* (Mākaro Press, 2017). He is a retired minister. His other interests are running and the ethics of climate change.

**Amanda Hunt** is a poet and environmental scientist from Rotorua. Her work has been published in *Landfall, takahē, Poetry New Zealand, Te Awa, Mimicry, Poems in the Waiting Room,* and on poetry and conservation websites and in numerous New Zealand Poetry Society anthologies. In 2016, she was shortlisted for the Sarah Broom Poetry Prize. Her work has been highly commended in several New Zealand Poetry Society International Competitions.

**Kevin Ireland** lives on Auckland's North Shore. His twenty-fifth book of poems, *Keeping a grip,* was published in 2018 by Steele Roberts Aotearoa. Kevin was awarded the Prime Minister's Award for Literary Achievement in 2004 and the A. W. Reed Award for Contribution to New Zealand Literature in 2006.

**Susan Jacobs** is a teacher, author and poet who lives in Auckland. She has written two non-fiction books (*Fighting with the Enemy* and *In Love and War,* Penguin 2003, 2012) about the Italian–New Zealand connection in World War II, and has worked as a lecturer, editor and book reviewer. Her poetry has been published in *Poetry New Zealand Yearbook 2018, takahē* and *Forty Years of Titirangi Poets* (2017). She teaches ESOL to adults, and is writing a novel.

**Maria Yeonhee Ji** is a writer and junior doctor based in Tāmaki Makaurau. She holds an MBChB and a BMedSci (Hons) from the University of Auckland, and dreams of adding a Master's in Creative Writing to this list. Her writing has appeared in several publications, including *The Pantograph Punch, takahē, Signals* and *Starling*.

**Ted Jenner** has published three books of poetry, one book of prose poems, short fiction and travel anecdotes, and two books of translations from ancient Greek poetry, including *The Gold Leaves*, messages for the dead inscribed on minute strips of gold foil. His latest book is *The Arrow that Missed* (Cold Hub Press, 2017).

**Gregory Kan**'s work has featured in literary journals such as *Atlanta Review, Cordite, Jacket, Landfall, New Zealand Listener, Sport* and *Best New Zealand Poems*, as well as art exhibitions, journals and catalogues. His first book of poetry, *This Paper Boat*, was shortlisted in the 2017 Ockham New Zealand Book Awards. Greg's most recent poetry collection, *Under Glass* (Auckland University Press), was published in 2019.

**Anne Kennedy** is a fiction writer, poet, screenplay editor and teacher. Her latest book is *Moth Hour* (Auckland University Press, 2019). In 2018, her novel *The Ice Shelf* was published by Victoria University Press. Her awards and residencies include the New Zealand Post Book Award for Poetry, the University of Iowa International Writers' Program Fall Residency (2017), and the IIML Writers' Residency (2016).

**Elizabeth (Libby) Kirkby-McLeod** is an Auckland author who has had poetry published in a range of New Zealand journals. She was long-listed for the 2008 *Six Pack 3* authors' anthology, and her poem 'Her

Warning Signs' was highly commended in the 2018 International Poetry Competition. Her first poetry collection, *Family Instructions Upon Release*, was published by The Cuba Press in 2019. She also has a children's book forthcoming with Gilt Edge Publishing.

**Elisabeth Kumar** is a lecturer in the University of Auckland School of Medicine's medical humanities programme, co-teaching (with Mike Hanne) a course called 'Unexamined Metaphors, Uncharted Stories'. She is particularly interested in literature around disability, madness and dialogue.

**Sarah Laing** is an award-winning cartoonist, short-story writer, novelist and graphic designer. Her fifth book, *Let me be Frank*, was published with Victoria University Press in 2019, and she has also illustrated children's books, made zines and co-edited *Three Words: An Anthology of Aotearoa/NZ Women's Comics*. Her most recent graphic memoir, *Mansfield and Me*, was long-listed in the 2017 Ockham New Zealand Book Awards, and was published in New Zealand and the United Kingdom, where it was favourably reviewed by *The Guardian* and *The Sunday Times Literary Supplement*.

**Jessica Le Bas** has published two collections of poetry, *incognito* (Auckland University Press, 2007) and *Walking to Africa* (Auckland University Press, 2009), and a novel for children, *Staying Home* (Penguin, 2010). She is the recipient of the 2019 Sarah Broom Poetry Prize, and currently lives in the Cook Islands.

**Wes Lee** lives in Paekakariki. She has two collections of poetry, *Shooting Gallery* (Steele Roberts Aotearoa, 2016) and *Body, Remember* (Eyewear Publishing, 2017). Her work has appeared in *The Stinging Fly, Poetry London, The London Magazine, Westerly, Mimicry, Turbine | Kapohau, Landfall, Going Down Swinging*, and *New Zealand Listener*, among others. She was selected as a finalist for the Sarah Broom Poetry Prize 2018, and awarded the Poetry New Zealand Prize 2019.

**Helen Lehndorf** is a writer and writing teacher. Her book *The Comforter* made the *New Zealand Listener*'s Top 100 Books of 2012. Her second book, about the practice of journalling, *Write to the Centre*, was published by Haunui Press in 2016. Her essay 'The Sensory Seeker' appeared in Massey University's 2017 anthology *Home*.

**Bronwyn Lloyd** is a crafter and writer who has published numerous catalogue essays and articles on New Zealand painting and applied art since 1999. Her first collection of short stories, *The Second Location*, was published by Titus books in 2011.

**Henry Ludbrook** is a Nelson-based poet. He is active in the Nelson Live Poets Group. He has appeared twice before in *Poetry New Zealand*. See his poetry blog called River Deliver Me: www.hello-hcludbrook.tumblr. com. It now has well over 110 poems on it.

**Courtney Sina Meredith** is an Auckland poet, playwright, fiction writer and musician. Her award-winning books include her play *Rushing Dolls*, poetry *Brown Girls in Bright Red Lipstick*, short stories *Tail of the Taniwha*, and her second children's book, *The Adventures of Tupaia*, which was published in 2019. Courtney has held various international residencies, including the International Writing Program at the University of Iowa, where she is an Honorary Fellow in Writing. She is the director of Tautai, New Zealand's leading contemporary Pacific arts trust.

**Fardowsa Mohamed** is a poet and doctor from Auckland. She has previous publications in *Landfall*, *Poetry New Zealand* and *The Spinoff*. Fardowsa is currently working on her first collection of poems.

**Leola Meynell** is a graduate student in psychology. She is passionate about women's rights and women's writing.

**Anuja Mitra** is a law and arts student at the University of Auckland. More of her work can be found in *Signals*, *Starling*, *Sweet Mammalian*,

*Mayhem* and *Three Lamps*, and was included in the 2017–2018 National Library exhibition 'The Next Word: Contemporary New Zealand Poetry'. She is co-founder of the new online arts platform *Oscen* at oscen.co.nz.

**Freda Morgan** is well past retirement age and has experience as a drama teacher and director of students' work. She has also worked in community drama *Mysteryplays* in Lincoln, England. Sometimes she works with church communities to express religious concepts in action. Poetry has come to her attention lately — that is, the writing of it. The cupboard is full of unpublished short stories, plays and, now, poetry.

**Elizabeth Morton** is published in New Zealand, Australia, Ireland, the United Kingdom, Canada and the United States. She was feature poet in the *Poetry New Zealand Yearbook 2017*, and is included in *Best Small Fictions 2016*. Her first poetry collection, *Wolf*, was published with Mākaro Press in 2017. She is completing a MLitt at the University of Glasgow, usually in her pyjamas.

**Art Nahill** is an Auckland physician and poet. His second collection, entitled *Murmurations*, was published in 2018.

**Elizabeth Nannestad** is an Auckland poet. She has had three books published: *Jump* (1985), *If he's a good dog he'll swim* (1996) and *Wild Like Me* (2013).

**Emma Neale** has published six novels and five poetry collections and edited several anthologies. Since 2018 she has been the editor of *Landfall*. Her latest collection of poetry is *To the Occupant* (Otago University Press, 2019).

**Janet Newman**'s poetry has been recognised by the International Writers Workshop Kathleen Grattan Award for a Sequence of Poems, the New Zealand Poetry Society Prize and the Caselberg Trust Poetry Prize. She is a PhD student in Creative Writing at Massey University. Her thesis explores New Zealand's long tradition of eco-poetry, and includes a collection of original poems.

**Bob Orr** was born in Waikato. Moving to Auckland, he worked as a seafarer on the Waitematā Harbour and Hauraki Gulf for 38 years. He now lives in a cottage on the Thames coast. His latest collection is *One Hundred Poems and a Year* (Steele Roberts Aotearoa, 2018).

**Robin Peace** has lived most of her life in Wellington. Her first full collection, *A Passage of Yellow Red Birds* (Mākaro Press), was published in 2018. She is currently enrolled in a Master's in Creative Writing at Massey University — shifting direction from an academic life as a geographer and evaluator. Home is now on the wetland margin of O te Pua on the Kāpiti coast.

**Sarah Penwarden** works as a therapist and counsellor educator in Auckland. She has had poems published in *Meniscus, Poetry New Zealand, Southerly, takahē* and *Turbine | Kapohau*. She has also had short stories published in *tākāhe* and *brief*, and a story broadcast on Radio New Zealand. Her writing for children has appeared in *The School Journal*.

**Joanna Preston** is a Tasmanaut poet, editor and freelance creative writing tutor who really is working on her second collection of poetry — 'this time I mean it, cross my heart and hope to die. Or at least finish the job.'

**essa may ranapiri** (takatāpui, they/them/theirs) has been writing poetry since 2007. They were born in Kirikiriroa in 1993, and have been living there since starting a BA in English at the University of Waikato in 2012. They have since completed a BA in English and History with Honours in English and a Master's in Creative Writing, which they received from IIML at Victoria University in Pōneke in 2017. Their first collection of poetry, *ransack* (Victoria University Press), was published in 2019.

**Vaughan Rapatahana** commutes between Hong Kong, the Philippines and Aotearoa New Zealand. He is widely published across several genres in both of his main languages, te reo Māori and English. He is a poet, with collections published in Hong Kong, Macau, the Philippines, the United States, England, France, India and New Zealand. *Atonement* was nominated for a National Book Award in Philippines (2016). He won the inaugural Proverse Poetry Prize the same year; and was included in *Best New Zealand Poems 2017*. In 2019 he performed at Poetry International, part of the London Literature Festival.

**Helen Rickerby** has published four books of poetry, most recently *How to Live* (Auckland University Press, 2019). She is interested in the elastic boundaries of what poetry can encompass, and has become especially obsessed with what happens when poetry and the essay meet and merge. She lives in Wellington, runs the boutique publishing company Seraph Press, and works a day job as an editor.

**Phoebe Robertson** is a former student of Katikati College.

**Jack Ross**'s latest book, *Ghost Stories*, was published by Lasavia Publishing in mid-2019. His previous novel, *The Annotated Tree Worship*, was highly commended in the fiction section of the 2018 NZSA Heritage Book Awards. He has been the managing editor of *Poetry New Zealand* since 2014. He blogs at http://mairangibay.blogspot.com/.

**Tim Saunders** farms sheep and beef near Palmerston North. He has had poetry and short stories published in *Turbine | Kapohau, takahē, New Zealand Listener* and *Flash Frontier*, and won the 2018 *Mindfood* magazine short story competition. He performs poetry around Manawatū and beyond.

**Eric Paul Shaffer** is author of seven books of poetry: *Even Further West; A Million-Dollar Bill; Lāhaina Noon; Portable Planet; Living at the Monastery, Working in the Kitchen; RattleSnake Rider;* and *Kindling:*

*Poems from Two Poets* (with James Taylor). More than 500 of his poems have been published in national and international reviews in Australia, Canada, Ireland, Japan, the Netherlands, New Zealand, Nicaragua and the United Kingdom. Shaffer received Hawai'i's 2002 Elliot Cades Award for Literature, a 2006 Ka Palapala Po'okela Book Award, and the 2009 James M. Vaughan Award for Poetry. Shaffer teaches composition, literature and creative writing at Honolulu Community College.

**Iain Sharp** is a retired manuscripts librarian who spends much of his time gazing contentedly across Nelson Haven toward the Western Ranges. He's the author of several poetry books and a biography of Charles Heaphy.

**Emma Shi** was the winner of the National Schools Poetry Award in 2013 and the Poetry New Zealand Prize in 2017. Her work was also included in *Best New Zealand Poems 2017*. Emma's poetry has been published in various literary journals such as *Landfall* and *Starling*. She is currently an editorial assistant at *a fine line*, the quarterly magazine of the New Zealand Poetry Society. Emma studied Classics at Victoria University of Wellington, and has lived in Wellington ever since. She writes at emmashi.co.nz.

**Jane Simpson** is a Christchurch-based poet, historian and tutor. In 2019 her second collection, *Tuning Wordsworth's Piano,* was published by Interactive Press, which also published *A world without maps* (2016), her first collection.

**Tracey Slaughter** is the author of the short-story collection *deleted scenes for lovers* (Victoria University Press, 2016*)*. Her poem 'breather' won second place in the international Peter Porter Poetry Prize 2018. Tracey's collection of poetry *Conventional Weapons* (Victoria University Press) was released in April 2019. She teaches at the University of Waikato, where she edits the literary journal *Mayhem*.

**Elizabeth Smither**'s latest publications are the poetry book *Night Horse* (Auckland University Press, 2017) and a novel, *Loving Sylvie* (Allen & Unwin, 2019). *Night Horse* won the 2018 Ockham New Zealand Book Awards Poetry Award, a prize which Elizabeth Smither has won three times.

**Michael Spring** is the author of four poetry books and one children's book. His poems have appeared in *Atlanta Review, Crannóg, Midwest Quarterly, Neon* and *Spillway*. Michael is a poetry editor for the *Pedestal Magazine*, and founding editor of Flowstone Press. He currently lives on a mountainside in rural Oregon, United States.

**Robert Sullivan** lives in Auckland with Rachel Fenton and their baby son, Turi. Sullivan's Māori tribal affiliations are to Ngāpuhi and Kāi Tahu. His PhD from the University of Auckland examines the work of five other indigenous Pacific poets. His seven collections of poetry include *Captain Cook in the Underworld, Shout Ha! to the Sky* and the bestselling *Star Waka*. He has co-edited three major anthologies of Pacific and Māori poetry.

**C. K. Stead** is an award-winning novelist, literary critic, poet and essayist. He was the New Zealand Poet Laureate from 2015 to 2017, has won the Prime Minister's Award for Fiction, and is a Member of the Order of New Zealand, the highest honour possible in New Zealand.

**Roger Steele** has published about 600 books, perhaps a third of them poetry, over the 22 years of Steele Roberts Aotearoa's existence. He still loves the stuff, but is trying to retire from publishing to focus more on golf, fishing and mokopuna. Particularly mokopuna.

**Hana Tawhai**, of Ngāti Porou, Ngāti Uepohatu and Pakēhā descent, first published at age eight, and workshopped with Margaret Mahy while in high school. She has written for teen and student magazines while attending Unitec, and Victoria and Massey universities. With tertiary qualifications in English, theatre, film and Māori Visual Arts, Hana is a multidisciplinary artist who specialises in spoken word, comedy and science fiction. She features in the recent *Hellfire Anthology 2017–2019* with a satirical commentary on pop-spiritual philosophies.

**Chris Tse** is the author of two collections of poetry published by Auckland University Press: *How to be Dead in a Year of Snakes* (winner of the Jessie Mackay Award for Best First Book of Poetry and a finalist at the 2016 Ockham New Zealand Book Awards) and *He's so MASC*. Along with Emma Barnes, Chris is currently editing an anthology of contemporary LGBTQIA+ Aotearoa New Zealand writers, to be published by Auckland University Press in early 2021.

**Bryan Walpert** is the author of three poetry collections, most recently *Native Bird* (Mākaro Press), as well as a short-story collection, and two scholarly books, most recently *Poetry and Mindfulness: Interruption to a Journey*. He is a professor in English and creative writing at Massey University, Auckland.

**Laura Williamson** is a writer based in Central Otago. She is the co-writer of *The Blue Moments Project* song and spoken word cycle, which premiered at the 2017 Festival of Colour, and her book *The Bike and Beyond: Life on Two Wheels in Aotearoa New Zealand* was published in 2016 as part of the BWB Text series from Bridget Williams Books.

**E Wen Wong** is a Year 13 student at Burnside High School in Christchurch.

**Sue Wootton** lives in Dunedin. Her novel, *Strip*, was long-listed in the 2017 Ockham New Zealand Book Awards, and her fifth poetry collection, *The Yield*, was a finalist in these awards in 2018. Sue edits the health humanities e-zine *Corpus: Conversations about Medicine and Life*. She is the 2020 Katherine Mansfield fellow in Menton.

**Dani Yourukova** is a local poet in Wellington, and an Honours student at Victoria University of Wellington. Their work has been featured in a handful of publications, most recently in *Mayhem, Aotearotica, takahē* and *Salty*.

**Karen Zelas** is a Christchurch writer, and the author of four books of poetry, most recently *The Trials of Minnie Dean*. She is working on a fifth.

**About
Poetry
New Zealand**

**Poetry New Zealand** is New Zealand's longest-running poetry magazine, showcasing new writing from this country and overseas. It presents the work of talented newcomers and developing writers as well as that of established leaders in the field.

Founded by Wellington poet Louis Johnson, who edited it from 1951 to 1964 as the *New Zealand Poetry Yearbook*, it was revived as a biennial volume by Frank McKay in 1971, a series which lasted until 1984. David Drummond (in collaboration with Oz Kraus's Brick Row Publishing) began to publish it again biannually in 1990. The journal reached its forty-eighth issue in 2014, the year Jack Ross of Massey University's School of English and Media Studies took it back to its roots by renaming it the *Poetry New Zealand Yearbook*.

*Poetry New Zealand* has been edited by some of New Zealand's most distinguished poets and academics, including Elizabeth Caffin, Grant Duncan, Riemke Ensing, Bernard Gadd, Leonard Lambert, Harry Ricketts, Elizabeth Smither and Brian Turner. The journal was overseen from 1993 to 2014 by celebrated poet, novelist, anthologist, editor and literary critic Alistair Paterson ONZM, with help from master printer John Denny of Puriri Press, and guest editors Owen Bullock, Siobhan Harvey and Nicholas Reid.

The magazine's policy is to support poetry and poets both in New Zealand and overseas. Each issue since 1994 has featured a substantial feature showcasing the work of a developing or established poet. It also includes a selection of poetry from New Zealand and abroad, as well as essays, reviews and critical commentary.

**Managing editor**
Jack Ross
editor@poetrynz.net

**Advisory board**

Thom Conroy
Jen Crawford
John Denny
Matthew Harris
Ingrid Horrocks
David Howard

Jan Kemp
Bronwyn Lloyd
Alistair Paterson
Tracey Slaughter
Bryan Walpert

**Website:** www.poetrynz.net
**Webmaster:** Warren Olds
**Blog:** poetrynzblog.blogspot.co.nz/
**index:** poetrynz.blogspot.co.nz/

**Submissions:** The submission dates for each issue are between 1 May and 31 July of each year. Submit either (preferably) by email, with your poems pasted in the body of the message or included as a MSWord file attachment; or by post, to the address below, with a stamped, self-addressed envelope, and contact details in your covering letter.

Dr Tracey Slaughter
English Programme
School of Arts
Waikato University
Private Bag 3105
Hamilton 3240

Please remember to include a short biography and current postal address with your submission. Each contributor will receive a free copy of the issue their work is included in.

# Index of new poems

First published in 2020 by Massey University Press
Private Bag 102904, North Shore Mail Centre
Auckland 0745, New Zealand
www.masseypress.ac.nz

Design by Jo Bailey
Typesetting by Megan van Staden

A catalogue record for this book is available from the
National Library of New Zealand

Printed and bound in China by Everbest Printing
Investment Limited

ISBN: 978-0-9951229-3-2

The assistance of Massey University's School of English
and Media Studies is gratefully acknowledged by the
publisher

The assistance of Creative New Zealand is gratefully
acknowledged by the publisher

ARTS COUNCIL OF NEW ZEALAND TOI AOTEAROA